Praise for *Be*

"Whether you're an entrepreneur, athlet
Be Unstoppable is your guide to achievin
your path. Alden's wisdom and actiona
an invitation to push beyond self-limitat
—Coach Lenny Van
and N

"Here are the lessons you want your chil
tion for personal fulfillment."
—L

"As a former US Army Special Forces op
neur, and a father, I highly recommend t
embedding the mission-critical compone
wonderful storyline that is both memor
your required reading list!"
—Larry Broughton, Fo

"Reading *Be Unstoppable* is like getting
except it's better. Mills removes the my
simple code that you can apply to anyt
This is a book that you will read over an
—A
World

"This book teaches what most people ir
However, knowing achieves nothing.
where this book scores so high. Throug
you to action."
—

"Alden infused this important work with
lenge for anyone looking for real change
ciples to my own business and life."
—David R. Duncan, President and

"I plan to read this to my daughter at le
to parents, and to anyone who wants to

"The bad news is that this book wasn't
The good news is that it will be mandat

BE
UNSTOPPABLE

Also by Alden Mills

Unstoppable Teams: The Four Essential Actions of High-Performance Leadership

Unstoppable Mindset: How to Use What You Have to Get What You Want

BE UNSTOPPABLE

The 8 Essential Actions to Succeed at Anything

ALDEN MILLS

Matt Holt Books
An Imprint of BenBella Books, Inc.
Dallas, TX

This book is designed to provide accurate and authoritative information about leadership and personal development. Neither the author nor the publisher is engaged in rendering legal, accounting, or other professional services by publishing this book. If any such assistance is required, the services of qualified professionals should be sought. The author and publisher will not be responsible for any liability, loss, or risk incurred as a result of the use and application of any information contained in this book.

First edition published 2013

Be Unstoppable copyright © 2025 by Alden Mills

All rights reserved. Except in the case of brief quotations embodied in critical articles or reviews, no part of this book may be used or reproduced, stored, transmitted, or used in any manner whatsoever, including for training artificial intelligence (AI) technologies or for automated text and data mining, without prior written permission from the publisher.

Matt Holt is an imprint of BenBella Books, Inc.
8080 N. Central Expressway
Suite 1700
Dallas, TX 75206
benbellabooks.com
Send feedback to feedback@benbellabooks.com

BenBella and *Matt Holt* are federally registered trademarks.

Printed in the United States of America
10 9 8 7 6 5 4 3 2 1

Library of Congress Control Number: 2025001596
ISBN 9781637747063 (hardcover)
ISBN 9781637747070 (electronic)

Editing by Lydia Choi
Copyediting by Kaya Skovdatter
Proofreading by Rebecca Maines and Lisa Story
Text design and composition by PerfecType, Nashville, TN
Interior illustrations by Dan Kirchoff
Printed by Sheridan MI
Quote on pages 87 and 138 is from Calvin Coolidge.
Quote on page 30 is by Ronald Reagan.
Quotes on pages 35 and 49 are by Henry Ford.
Quote on pages 52 and 53 is from Benjamin Franklin.
Quote on page 52 is by Louis Pasteur.
Quote on page 79 is by Nikos Kazantzakis.

Special discounts for bulk sales are available. Please contact bulkorders@benbellabooks.com.

*For our Captains-in-Training,
H-master, Chow, Bear, and Yummy:
Be Unstoppable at going after your dreams!
Love, Mom and Dad*

AUTHOR'S NOTE

The story in this book is a work of fiction. Names, characters, places, and incidents are either the product of my imagination or used fictitiously. Any resemblance to actual persons, living or dead, business establishments, events, or locales is entirely coincidental.

*"Go confidently in the direction of your dreams!
Live the life you've imagined."
—Henry David Thoreau*

*"The future belongs to those
who believe in the beauty of their dreams."
—Eleanor Roosevelt*

CONTENTS

Foreword | xiii

Introduction | 1

Prologue to a Sea Story | 6

Action #1   **U**nderstand the Why | 26

Action #2   **P**lan in 3-D | 46

Action #3   **E**xercise to Execute | 60

Action #4   **R**ecognize Your Reason to Believe | 76

Action #5   **S**urvey Your Habits | 94

Action #6   **I**mprovise | 108

Action #7   **S**eek Expert Advice | 126

Action #8   **T**eam Up | 134

Acknowledgments | 155

FOREWORD

When you watch someone transform the mindset and trajectory of your 13-year-old son in a matter of hours, it becomes very personal. It's one thing to read a book, listen to an amazing keynote, and become dear friends with someone—but it's quite another when you witness the impact of their approach with your child. This is my story of how I experienced this book in real life.

Ten years ago, a member of my Entrepreneurs' Organization forum asked if we could invite some new expats to a family barbeque we were hosting at our home in Barcelona. Those guests were Alden Mills, a former Navy SEAL, and his family. At that time, he had just sold his business after a 10-year Scaling Up journey.

As our families mingled, Alden and I discovered we shared a purpose in helping people follow their dreams and achieve their goals. He and his lovely wife, Jennifer—who, like us, have four children—also shared our determination to pass along our love of international travel and learning from other cultures.

Fast-forward five years and our families had become dear friends. My youngest son, Quinn, was taking part in a rites of passage experience my pastor helped us design for our children. As Alden was a former platoon commander and mentor to Quinn, I sought his help on a weekend dedicated to strengthening Quinn's physical and mental well-being.

Alden designed a sunrise hike in the Marin Headlands of Northern California that included a half-dozen false summits. Quinn, who wasn't accustomed to activities like this, lagged from the beginning.

"Hustle up here, Quinn," was one of the first things I heard as we embarked on our journey. Alden had summoned Quinn to the front while coaching him on mindset training. The stories he told and the practical tools he shared kept Quinn's focus on learning and away from the steep climb he was experiencing.

I watched, somewhat surprised, as my son shifted his perspective and ended up beating all of us up a difficult two-hour climb and back down, with no complaints. I remember Quinn's mother exclaiming, when he returned, that he'd been transformed from a young insecure boy to a confident young man overnight. Quinn subsequently developed a love of physical activity and embraced, as Alden would say, "an Unstoppable Mindset," which he continues to exude today.

Shortly after that early morning climb, Alden asked me for an endorsement of the second edition of *Be Unstoppable*. I did not hesitate. My description of his book was simple and to the point: "Timeless and transformative. READ THIS BOOK." I have witnessed Alden in action not only with my son but on our Scaling Up stages across the country. From his speaking to his coaching, he lives by the lessons in this book.

> If you are a parent seeking another voice to inspire your child to get out of their comfort zone: READ THIS BOOK.
>
> If you are thinking of making a career change to do something new and exciting: READ THIS BOOK.
>
> If you are considering throwing caution to the wind to chase your dream: READ THIS BOOK.
>
> Or
>
> If you just want to be inspired to live a little bit better: READ THIS BOOK.

Be Unstoppable will recondition how you think about what you want in life, what's holding you back, and how to achieve it; arming you with several useful tools to help you and the ones you love keep pursuing their dreams. You'll have a chance to experience the lessons that made a lasting impact on my son and led me to invite Alden to open for General Stanley McChrystal, who keynoted our *Fortune* magazine Growth Summit. Alden's impact has since spread to our tribe of growing firms.

As H. Jackson Brown Jr.'s mother once wrote:

Twenty years from now you will be more disappointed by the things you didn't do than by the ones you did. So, throw off the bowlines, sail away from the safe harbor. Catch the trade winds in your sails. Explore.

If you sense it's your time to set sail, or know someone ready to leave the comfort zone of their safe harbor, I promise you the next few hours of reading will be worth it.

—Verne Harnish, Founder of Entrepreneurs' Organization (EO) and Scaling Up, and author of *Scaling Up (Rockefeller Habits 2.0)*

INTRODUCTION

My inspiration and purpose for writing this book comes from my boys—all four of them. As their mother and I proudly watch them grow and test our patience by purposely not listening to our spoken words, I'm hopeful the written word might have more lasting impact. Like most parents, we want our children to succeed. We want to give them the tools for success, including a good education and a full array of life skills from swimming to not hitting their brothers to flossing their teeth. As we navigate parenthood without a map or playbook, life doesn't wait for us to adapt; it just happens.

A lot has happened since I made the decision to leave the SEAL teams and start my own business. For starters, several of my SEAL teammates are no longer with us. Back then we prepared "just-in-case" letters to be sent to our loved ones if we didn't return from a mission. In mine, I would thank my parents for the gifts they had given me, which enabled me to do what I loved doing most at that moment: leading SEALs. I would tell them not to be upset—that if the letter had been sent, it meant that I had died doing what I loved, and how many people are privileged to say that? I always wrote a letter to my younger brother, Andrew, usually starting it with a laundry list of apologies. Sorry for throwing a rock at your head in third grade, sorry for pretending to drown you at the lake, sorry for breaking your favorite Matchbox cars, and (the one I will always regret most) sorry for missing your wedding. But I always tried to end on a positive note, telling him how proud of him I was for following his rowing dreams, and that he could do anything he put his mind to. I would tell him to keep trying, to never give up, and to know that even though I was no longer physically there for him I would always be with him in spirit, cheering him on.

Thankfully, none of my letters ever needed to be sent. But that hasn't been the case for many SEAL teammates. Such was the situation with Petty Officer First Class Neil Roberts, the first Navy SEAL to die in Afghanistan. Neil was a friend, training classmate, and a former sister platoonmate, and when he died on March 2, 2002, I knew that a letter was going to an 18-month-old son. While grieving Neil's death, I found myself wondering what he had written to his child. During this time of reflection, my wife became pregnant. Her pregnancy and Neil's death inspired me to write a "just-in-case" letter to my soon-to-be child. It wasn't a particularly good letter—more like a list of "do's and don'ts." I felt that it wasn't quite right, that it was too preachy and not very memorable. The busyness of life got in the way of editing it until we were blessed with another pregnancy, which inspired me toward a rewrite. This process would repeat over the next ten years with the birth of my four boys. Even after Yummy (William) was born, the letter still wasn't great, but with my wife's encouragement and on an anniversary trip to Hawaii together, I outlined what would become this book.

Back in those SEAL days I had the confidence of knowing I could do anything I put my mind to. I wanted this book to capture those themes in a way my boys and everyone else who reads it would remember. A collection of vignettes could illustrate how anyone can accomplish great things, but would it leave a lasting impression? So I tried to create a framework, a code my sons can follow throughout their lives, a touchstone to encourage them when the going gets tough. I want this book to capture the essence of my spirit as a tangible reference for them, a pick-me-up when they feel like giving up on a dream, a voice of encouragement when no one else believes in them, or perhaps simply the voice of a proud father saying, "Go for it—you can do it!"

I've spent the better part of the last ten years thinking about what this book should be. In the end I settled on three ideas to make it memorable and, hopefully, inspire others to go after their dreams. The first idea was to decipher and distill the essence of how I was able to beat asthma, become a rowing champion, lead Navy SEALs, and create the fastest-growing consumer products company in the United States (in 2009). What I realized by analyzing these pivotal successes in my life was that in each of them I unknowingly put eight actions into motion. Over time I refined those actions into a simple, easy-to-remember code called U.P.E.R.S.I.S.T., as explained in the eight chapters of this book.

The second challenge was determining how to teach the code in a memorable way without losing the reader (my boys and you) in the process. I decided that a parable would offer the most memorable and engaging way to introduce the code, and what better way to build a connection with the reader and the code than to use the metaphor of a captain and his ship? (Sorry, Army fans, but Navy wins on this one. If you prefer a land-based metaphor, simply replace the word "ship" with "tank.")

The final component was to provide readers with the ability to implement each of the eight actions immediately. There's no time like the present to start making your dreams happen, and this book should encourage you to take action ASAP! This is the reasoning behind the "How to Get Started" section at the end of each chapter. I include short insights into my SEAL and entrepreneurial experiences in each of these eight sections to help demonstrate how these actions can work for anyone going after their dreams.

Speaking of dreams, if you remember nothing else from this book, remember this: "YOUR LIFE IS UP TO YOU. YOU DECIDE WHAT KIND OF LIFE YOU LIVE!"

Those words, I now realize, have guided me over the course of my life. I decided not to listen to the doctor who said that, due to my asthma, I should learn to play chess instead of playing outside. I decided to work harder so I could pull harder than other rowers and earn the opportunity to win a gold medal at the New England Championships and the Olympic Festival. I decided not to quit when more than 80% of my classmates rang out of SEAL training. I decided to invent the Perfect Pushup when my investors told me to get a job. In each of my most important successes in life, the key was not giving up on a dream. And the key to not giving up on a dream is understanding why you want to make that dream come true. The better you understand your "why," the better able you will be to persist when others give up on you. Understanding your "why" also lets you figure out your way. Once you do, you'll come to appreciate that we have only two limitations in life: our ability to dream and the courage to follow those dreams.

Dreaming isn't difficult (especially when you're young). It's the follow-up that's hard, and that's where I know this book will come in handy. The sad truth is that few dreams ever become reality. Why? The answer is in your head: Your mind can be your best friend or your worst enemy, and it's the deciding factor for the kind of life you live. Your mind isn't pre-programmed to tell you what to do with the dreams it conjures. Your mind is only as good as the inputs it receives. If the chief input is a constant stream of "you can't," then your dream is dead on arrival. But if the inputs streaming in begin with "What if . . . ?" and "You can!" your dreams have a chance of becoming real. And the most important inputs, the ones that matter most, are the ones your mind gives itself.

Unfortunately, essential though it is, the power of positive input isn't all you need to succeed. Your master and commander, your mind, needs more to be convinced to work at making a dream real.

This book gives your mind a code to follow so that no matter what obstacles attempt to derail you, your mind will be working for you, not against you. And when your mind is on your side, no obstacle is too big, no dream too daunting, and nothing can stop you from living an amazing life!

Once you've mastered the code in this book, your biggest challenge will be dreaming bigger! Because once you've tasted success and gained confidence from making a dream come true, a funny thing happens—you get addicted to making even more dreams come true. And as each dream gets a little bigger and a little scarier, you get stronger, smarter, and better at reaching them. And isn't that what life is all about? Live your dreams!

Dream on, boys, you can do it!

I love you,
Dad

PROLOGUE TO
A SEA STORY

The town of Uptoyou is unique. Every resident owns a boat. From oldest to youngest, each person gets a boat the day they are born, and they keep it until the day they die. Their lives are spent learning how to captain their boats. These boats are unlike any you can buy; each one is slightly different—unique to the individual—but all function the same.

Uptoyou boats grow with their owners and can be modified over time. They can be made faster, bigger to carry more, or tougher to handle

bigger seas. But modifications take time and commitment—the bigger the change, the longer the wait.

All children born in Uptoyou attend Uptoyou University, where they learn how to be captains. They study the basics of seamanship and navigation: how to drive, maintain, and improve their boats, as well as how to make a living with them. By the time they graduate, they're ready to test their skills in one of the busiest ports in the world, Hardwork Harbor.

It's where all the people of Uptoyou go to work and play. From ferries and cargo boats to explorers, Hardwork Harbor has a place for everyone's boat.

Recently, two boys named Tim and Ted graduated from Uptoyou University. They grew up on the same street and had been friends as long as they could remember. Both dreamed of high adventure, captaining their boats around the globe in search of fun, fortune, and fame.

Though they had attended the same school and earned the same degree, Tim and Ted weren't the same. Nothing came easy for Tim. He often felt life was unfair because he had to work harder than Ted at nearly everything—whether getting good grades or boating on the water.

Ted loved to talk about everything he did. He boasted about how easy it all was for him. He bragged about what he would do after leaving university—travel the world in his boat, invent things everyone needed, and become rich and famous. No one doubted Ted; he made everything look easy, and it seemed inevitable he would succeed in Hardwork Harbor.

Ted was popular and had many friends. Tim wasn't nearly as popular, but he still called Ted a friend. Tim had dreams too, but he kept them to himself, afraid others would laugh at his ambitions of sailing the seven seas—especially since he had barely passed the university navigation exams.

When they finally graduated, Ted won the award for most likely to succeed in Hardwork Harbor. Tim didn't win any awards, but they both earned their degrees and became captains.

Their first weeks of work were exciting. They started with the same job: ferrying cargo from one side of the harbor to the other. Tim found the work challenging but rewarding. He worked hard to keep up with the other boats while learning to navigate Hardwork Harbor's waters, which were much harder to manage than those he'd studied in school. Every week brought new challenges. Sandbars constantly shifted, and winds and waves never stayed the same, making it difficult for the captains to carry their loads.

Tim loved the challenge. No two days were the same. Ted, on the other hand, grew frustrated. Just as he thought he had mastered the best route, he had to relearn it the next week. He was destined for greatness—everyone at school had told him so. Why should someone like him be stuck doing a lowly cargo job when he should be navigating the high seas with precious cargo bound for foreign harbors?

After a few weeks, the young captains met with the older captains of the cargo company. The seasoned captains offered advice—from how to carry cargo more efficiently to how to read the waters to avoid running aground. Tim listened carefully, taking notes and asking questions. He respected their experience, knowing it would help him improve.

Ted didn't think he needed their help. Some of these captains hadn't even graduated from Uptoyou University, let alone won awards like Ted had. What could they possibly know that he didn't?

As the weeks turned into months, something interesting began to happen. At first, it was barely noticeable, but every so often Tim would finish his cargo run before Ted, even though they carried identical loads over the same routes. Tim had never beaten Ted at *anything* before. Ted had always been first at everything—as he liked to remind Tim. But now things were changing.

On the days Tim finished first, he never mentioned it. Ted, however, always found ways to take credit for Tim's success. He made sure to talk about it only when other captains were within earshot, saying he'd slowed to save fuel or stopped to chat with another captain.

After a year, Tim consistently finished his work before Ted. The older captains took notice and offered Tim more responsibility: a new course with heavier cargo. As word spread, Ted began telling anyone who'd listen that the senior captains didn't like him, that they were *jealous* of his natural abilities. He insisted that was why he wasn't given the bigger loads or longer routes. He even told Tim the only reason he got the new route was because the older captains felt sorry for him.

While Ted made excuses, Tim made changes to his boat to handle the increased workload. He needed to make it bigger and stronger to carry more cargo and manage the longer course. It wasn't easy. Tim struggled to navigate his boat with the heavier load and often spent weekends practicing his docking skills or testing new navigation methods to manage deeper waters. Adapting his boat was exciting, but it was also frustrating, frightening, and a lot of work.

Tim had just gotten comfortable with his expanded cargo course when the older captains offered him a chance to navigate a route across the bay to the North. This made Tim nervous. It had taken nearly a year to master the east-west route across Hardwork Harbor, and the new course required northerly headings. Only a small portion of his old route would overlap with the new one, and navigating the bay would mean taking seas broadside—a first for Tim.

In the nights leading up to his departure he tossed and turned, mind filled with questions: How long would it take to master this new course? Would he even make it? What if he ran his boat aground? What if it sank? The questions wouldn't stop, and all he could focus on were the things that could go wrong. By the time the departure day arrived, Tim was an anxious wreck.

The day he ran the new course turned out to be the worst of his life on the water. Ted and his group of friends showed up, supposedly to wish him luck—but their smirks made it clear they were there to see him fail.

Tim was so nervous when he motored away from the pier that he forgot to untie a dock line. The result was a parted line, a bent cleat, and a harbor full of laughter from Ted and his friends.

Once he left them behind, Tim began to relax. The first leg of the route was familiar—he had navigated it the entire previous year. But soon, he turned onto a new heading and entered unfamiliar waters. At first, it seemed manageable, then the winds shifted and the seas grew rougher. Waves began crashing over the port side.

The boat shuddered and wallowed as it plowed into one wave after another. Tim panicked. He had never encountered conditions like this and feared his boat wouldn't hold up. He found himself repeating aloud the questions that had haunted him during his sleepless nights.

Lost in his panic, Tim stopped paying attention to his navigation. By the time he realized he had slipped out of the channel, it was too late. He spotted the sandbar on the starboard side just as his bow scraped into the hard sand.

Tim tried to reverse off the sandbar, but with broadside seas and a heavy cargo, his engines weren't strong enough to free the boat.

Tim sat trembling on the bridge for several minutes, trying to avoid what he knew he had to do: make a distress call. He was less worried about getting off the sandbar than about the entire harbor hearing his call for help. He was certain it would ruin his chances with the cargo company, and he dreaded the teasing he'd endure from Ted and his followers. His stomach churned as he made the call: "This is Captain Tim requesting . . . ah . . . assistance, over." His voice was weak and uncertain as it echoed over the radio channel that all harbor captains monitored.

"Captain Tim, this is Captain Bill. Please advise what kind of assistance is required, over." It was the same captain who had given him the new course. Tim was crushed. It took him a full minute to stammer a reply: "Ah . . . ah . . . a . . . tow."

Captain Bill didn't hesitate. He requested Tim's location and confirmed that he was on his way. It took two hours for Bill to arrive, and during the wait Tim kept trying to free his boat by revving the engines. But it was in vain, And by the time Captain Bill arrived, Tim had damaged his propellers. He now needed a tow not just off the sandbar, but all the way to his destination.

Captain Bill kept their radio transmissions brief as they coordinated the tow, but even with minimal chatter, word spread to Ted and his buddies about what had happened.

To make matters worse, while Tim was under tow he had to keep his shipboard radio on to communicate with Captain Bill. This also meant enduring Ted and his shipmates' relentless quips about the incident. Tim felt this was the worst day of his life. He didn't want to leave his boat and even wondered how long he could live onboard to avoid facing other captains. Maybe he could drop anchor in the middle of the bay, as some captains had done, and only row ashore at night to get provisions, avoiding as many people as possible.

As Captain Bill towed him to a berth, Tim continued plotting ways to hide from the other captains. When they arrived, he was too upset to look Bill in the eye or thank him. He hurriedly untied the towline from his bow, and the older captain, without a word, tipped his cap at Tim before heading back to the south end of Hardwork Harbor.

Tim hid on the bridge, watching as his cargo was unloaded. The late-afternoon sun cast its light across the bay when a ship silently glided into the slip beside his. At first, Tim didn't want to look, afraid he might make eye contact with the other captain and face more ridicule. But that thought quickly faded.

The hardware and brightwork of the approaching vessel gleamed as though a signaling mirror were capturing the sun's rays. The reflection was so dazzling that Tim had to shield his eyes. As his vision adjusted, his jaw dropped, and he rose to get a better view of the magnificent ship.

Momentarily forgetting his sadness, Tim stared in awe at the most incredible vessel he had ever seen. The stainless steel railings, cleats, horns, bells, anchors, capstans, and portholes reflected the light brilliantly. But there was more—the ship's high-flared bow was coated in onyx black marine paint, with a bloodred stripe where the hull met the water.

Tim's eyes danced from stem to stern, taking in every detail of the ship. Massive satellite domes rose above the bridge, and matching anchors adorned both bow and stern. Oiled teak decks and varnished handrails gleamed in the sunlight, and the graceful hull lines flowed like waves from bow to stern. She was a masterpiece.

Tim stood in silence, mouth agape and eyes wide, as the captain expertly maneuvered the ship into the slip. He couldn't believe such a vessel even existed, let alone that it was moored just one slip away from his own.

Tim stood in a daze on his bridge, staring at the large, brass-colored letters arcing across the teak transom of the ship: *Persistence*. Lost in daydreams about the ship's capabilities, he almost missed the captain's hearty call: "Ahoy there, captain!"

What Tim saw

Tim glanced awkwardly behind him, thinking, *He couldn't be speaking to me, could he?* Finally, he replied with a crackle in his voice, "Ahh, ahoy, sir."

The captain of the *Persistence* was much older than Tim but spoke with youthful energy. "Say, captain, I've been at sea for months and haven't been back to Hardwork Harbor in years. Are you from around here?"

Caught off guard by the captain's eagerness to chat, Tim fumbled his response. "No. I . . . I mean . . . yes." He flushed with embarrassment and tried to clarify. "I . . . I . . . I'm from Hardwork Harbor, on the southern side of the bay. It's my first visit to the northern side."

"Well, welcome to Hardwork Harbor North!" the captain said with a smile. "Say, do you like fried clams and chowder?"

Tim tilted his head slightly, as if to say, *Who doesn't?* But all he managed was a slow nod and a quiet, "Sure."

"Great! There's a clam shack at the end of the pier with the best food this side of the harbor. How about joining me? I'd love to hear what's been happening in Hardwork Harbor!" The senior captain smiled warmly, waiting for a response.

Tim muttered quietly to himself, "Where have you been all those years? I've never met someone who's left Hardwork Harbor for so long." A question popped into his head: *Why would a captain of such a grand ship want to spend time with someone like me? Surely, he won't once he finds out I was the one who ran aground today.*

As Tim nodded, the captain called out, "Terrific! I'll meet you on the pier in five minutes."

Tim froze—he had accidentally said yes! He had never been to dinner with someone so important. His mind raced: *What will I talk about? What will he think when he finds out I hit a sandbar?* Tim considered making up an excuse to stay on his boat, but then he heard the captain walking up the gangway.

"Hiya, captain! Name's Peter. Mind if I come aboard for a minute? I used to have a boat just like this one!"

Shell-shocked, Tim extended his hand, receiving a firm, energetic handshake. "Hi, sir. I'm, ah . . . Tim. Welcome aboard, sir." Tim felt small in the presence of such an impressive captain.

Peter grinned. "What's all this 'sir' business? We're both captains! Please, call me Peter."

Peter asked for a tour of Tim's boat and peppered him with questions about everything—from the harbor to the modifications Tim had made. Peter seemed genuinely interested in what Tim had to say and even complimented his boat! Tim couldn't believe it. For the first time that day he felt himself relax, and with newfound confidence he asked, "Could I tour your boat, too?"

"Of course, Tim! I'd be delighted to give you a tour of the *Persistence*."

The invitation lit a spark in Tim. It was as if he became a different person—his excitement contagious. Peter smiled warmly at the young captain as they stepped aboard the *Persistence*.

Tim couldn't believe his eyes. This was the most magnificent boat he had ever set foot on. Everything about it was incredible. The inlaid teak decks gleamed, and massive anchors were attached to automated stainless steel winches. Her decks were protected by the highest flared bow Tim had ever seen.

As he toured the bow, Tim noticed large steel plates welded to the hull. He imagined how easily this boat would have handled the waves he had battled earlier that day.

As the tour continued, Tim noticed other unusual modifications, such as a massive engine connected to an equally massive anchor on the stern. In the engine room were two diesel engines linked to rows of batteries, and on the bridge were more electronic systems than Tim had ever imagined. Peter showed him a radar system that could spot ships over the horizon, a sonar system that detected submerged obstacles hundreds of meters ahead, and a night vision system that allowed a captain to see a mile in any direction, even on the darkest nights.

Tim couldn't help but daydream about the *Persistence*'s incredible capabilities. The more he learned, the more he wondered how he could turn his own boat into a ship like this. Peter had spent a lifetime improving his boat, and it showed—the *Persistence* was prepared for anything.

As they moved into the wardroom and galley, Tim was captivated by the exotic artifacts displayed on the walls. There were handmade spears, animal figurines carved from bone and stone, colorful paintings of distant lands with snow-white beaches and turquoise waters teeming with brilliant fish, hand-woven baskets, and elegant wooden bowls. One painting depicted a captain and ship battling a ferocious storm, so lifelike it seemed to leap off the wall.

Peter's wardroom felt more like a gallery of fine art than a dining room, and Tim was overwhelmed with curiosity.

Noticing Tim's astonishment, Peter broke the silence. "You know, Tim, I grew up in Uptoyou too. I had a boat just like yours at your age, and I even did the same job you're doing now."

"Really?" Tim asked, dumbfounded. "I've never seen a boat like yours in the harbor before."

"Tim, have you ever left Hardwork Harbor?"

"I've thought about it, but I haven't yet," Tim admitted sheepishly.

"That's understandable. I didn't leave until I was older than you. It took me a long time to build up the courage. I'll never forget how everyone told me I was crazy—that I'd wreck my boat somewhere far away or be swallowed by a sea monster. It seems funny now, but back then it terrified me."

Tim knew exactly what Peter was talking about. Although he hadn't told anyone about his dream, he could imagine the ridicule he'd face—especially after how they treated him when he ran aground. Tim nodded slowly at Peter's confession and asked, "So why did you leave?"

Peter grinned as they headed back to the pier. "One night I was working late on my boat, making repairs—I'd run aground earlier that day—"

"You ran aground too?" Tim nearly shouted in astonishment.

Peter laughed heartily. "If I had a dollar for every time I ran aground, I'd be the richest man in Hardwork Harbor! I did it so often my so-called friends gave me a helmet so I wouldn't hurt myself on the bridge. My motto is: if you don't run aground now and then, you're not trying hard enough!"

Tim stood slack-jawed as Peter's words sank in. Peter chuckled and said, "C'mon, sailor, let's go get some chowder and fried clams. I'm starving!"

Peter was halfway down the gangway before Tim scrambled to follow. Peter's quick pace surprised Tim—he certainly walked with a spring in his step for an older captain. They continued in comfortable silence, taking in the waterfront sights as they made their way to Jack's Clam Shack.

Inside the dilapidated restaurant, covered with lobster pot buoys, Peter closed his eyes, took a deep sniff, and smiled. "Smells just the way

I remember it!" Turning to Tim, he said, "A cup of clam chowder and the fried-clam platter is the only way to go, skipper."

Tim, still taking in the restaurant's surroundings and scanning for a menu, replied, "Ah, sounds good to me. Count me in for the same."

While Captain Peter ordered, Tim finally spotted the menu. It was scratched in white chalk on a green board resting on two lobster pots:

Chowdah—made fresh daily
Full-belly Clams only
Lobstah when we have it—we don't have it
All meals come with fries and slaw—no substitutions
Cash Only: If you have to ask how much, then this isn't the place
for you.
Jack

Tim was struck by how short and curt the menu was, and was about to comment on it when Peter said, "Isn't it great? Simple and to the point. Good old Captain Jack knew exactly what he wanted when he built this place. I love it—totally authentic, just like Jack!"

Tim nodded slowly and muttered under his breath, "Yep, definitely one of a kind."

Just then, a booming voice bellowed, "Shiver me clam shells, look what the tide brought in: P-Squared!"

Jack's Clam Shack

A mountain of a man leaned over the counter to embrace Captain Peter. He wore a white apron, now stained brown from years of fryer grease and clam batter. His hands and forearms, dusted in flour, revealed faded tattoos beneath the smudges. He grabbed Peter in a massive bear hug.

"So good to see you, Jack!" Peter exclaimed, hugging him back.

"How many moons has it been, P2? Twelve at least!" Jack said, gripping Peter's shoulders to get a good look at him.

"Sixteen by my count. Couldn't make it any longer—started going into chowdah and fried clam withdrawals!" Peter grinned with a wink. Turning toward Tim, he added, "Jack, I'd like you to meet a first timer to your fine establishment. Meet Tim."

"Ahoy there, Tim! Good to meet ya. Hope you brought your appetite, 'cause you're in for a treat tonight!" Jack said, engulfing Tim's hand in his and squeezing hard enough to make him wince.

As Jack led them to a table in front of an old mahogany ship's wheel paired with a brass compass—clearly a place of honor—he flashed a toothy grin. "So, Double-P, what brings ya in? Surely you've reverse-engineered my secret clam batter recipe by now."

Peter gave Jack a warm tap on the shoulder. "Jack, old Double-P here gave up on cracking your recipe a long time ago. You've got nothing to worry about—that's one recipe Pierre-deuce will never master. As for what brings me in, I need to make a little tweak to the *Persistence*. I hear the boys down the pier might be able to make her just a bit less thirsty."

Jack nodded slowly, chuckling. "You never change, do you, old boy? Still making improvements?"

Peter gave a slight nod. Jack turned to Tim and said, "Son, soak up every word this captain offers you." Jack's jovial tone shifted to seriousness, startling Tim. "My chowdah and clams may be the best, but there's no skipper finer than the one sitting next to you right now."

Tim sat up straighter in his chair and replied, "Aye, aye, Jack."

"That's the spirit. Keep that attitude, and you just might learn something that'll change your life," Jack said, leaning in as if sharing a secret.

Satisfied that his message had been received, Jack turned his attention back to Peter.

"Well, my friend, all's good here. Still living the dream, as I'm sure you are. I'd love to stay and chat, but I've got clams to fry! Promise me you'll stop by before lunch tomorrow so we can catch up on your latest courses. Promise me, P-P!" Jack demanded, standing firm until Peter agreed.

Peter smiled. "Have I ever left without saying goodbye, my old friend?"

"Point taken. Now, make sure the youngster here doesn't fill up on oyster crackers before the best meal of his life arrives!" the proud chef called as he walked away.

New questions whirled through Tim's mind: What was with all the nicknames for Peter? And how could listening to Peter change his life? Before he could ask, Peter gave him a knowing look and said, "I love his energy—always upbeat. And I promise you'll love his food."

Tim nodded. "He's definitely fired up. I've never met anyone so passionate about chowder and clams."

"That's what makes this place special, Tim. I'm not kidding when I say captains from around the globe detour just to have a meal at Jack's Shack. Do you know why?"

"He uses a special batter recipe and fresh clams?" Tim guessed.

"Great ingredients help, but that's not the real reason captains change their course. It's because Jack loves what he does. You can't fake that kind of passion—it's contagious. People want to be around someone like him. He finds joy in serving the very best chowder and fried clams. That's his course, and people want to come along for the ride," Peter explained.

Tim leaned forward nervously on the old wooden table and slowly nodded, trying to absorb what Peter had just said. Peter could tell from Tim's body language that the message wasn't fully sinking in, so he took a different approach.

"Okay, let's get back to the topic we started before my stomach interrupted us: running aground."

At this, Tim shot upright in his chair. "You've really run aground more than once?"

Peter leaned back and laughed out loud. "*Yes.*" He leaned forward, resting a hand on Tim's shoulder, and continued. "The way I see it, the important thing about running aground is understanding *why* it happened. Once you know the 'why,' you'll figure out the 'way' to avoid it—at least on that leg of the course."

"I'm not sure I follow, Peter. What do you mean by the 'why' and the 'way'?"

Peter nodded. "Understanding the 'why' is the single most important thing a captain can do. And it's not just about running aground—it applies to everything. Knowing the 'why' behind what you're doing gives you the purpose to accomplish anything you want. It's what keeps you going when everyone else gives up. Once you understand the 'why,' you can start working on the 'way' to get it done."

He paused for a moment, then added, "Look, Tim, I ran aground so many times because I was trying new courses or pushing to do something a little better, a little faster than the other captains. My boat wasn't as fast or strong as theirs, so the only way I could keep up was by finding new, shorter routes. Sometimes it worked—most of the time it didn't. But here's the real key: Why was I pushing myself so hard in the first place? A lot of my friends thought I was foolish. They didn't understand why I was willing to take those risks."

Tim interrupted. "So why *were* you?"

Peter smiled. "Well, that goes back to what happened after I ran aground for the first time. I met a captain—actually, she was more than a captain, though I didn't realize it at the time."

"Huh?" Tim said. "I didn't know there was anything above a captain."

"There is, Tim. It's called a 'master and commander.' Technically, we're all captains, but a master and commander takes orders from no one. They've become so skilled at running their ship that they don't need the support of a fleet. Masters and commanders are so good they can find work anywhere they cruise."

"I had no idea you could do that. Are there a lot of them?"

"Yes, but don't worry that you haven't met any. They don't travel in fleets—or even with other captains. They follow their own courses," Peter explained. "Though many of them make a habit of stopping at Jack's," he added with a wink.

"Now, as I was saying," Peter continued, "I was sulking around the harbor after running aground for the first time when I saw a ship like nothing I'd ever seen before. It coasted into the berth right next to mine, and much like how you and I met, I met a friendly older captain who goes by 'Mother B.'

"She noticed my interest in her ship and invited me aboard. I asked her all kinds of questions but mostly just marveled at her ship and the places it had taken her—seemingly all around the world, to places I'd never even heard of. That night, I knew I wanted to live a life like hers, and I told her so."

Tim leaned forward eagerly. "What did she say?"

"That I was in luck—anyone can become a master and commander. But she warned me only a few ever do."

"How come?"

"Because they won't follow the Master and Commander Code."

"What code?!" Tim exclaimed, nearly falling out of his chair. Peter sat back, smiling, as he saw himself in Tim—thirty years younger, asking the same excited question.

"Calm down and listen. I'll tell you, but only on one condition."

Tim could hardly contain himself. He interrupted Peter—now clearly revealed as a master and commander—for the third time in under a minute. "Name it! I want to be a master and commander too!"

"I believe you," Peter said, leaning forward slowly and locking eyes with Tim. The intensity startled him. He couldn't help feeling that Peter was peering directly into his soul.

"The condition is simple. Tell me what you're willing to give up to follow the code."

Tim blinked, caught off guard. "What do you mean?"

"For starters, most of your friends. Not all of them—just the ones who aren't true friends. You'll be lonely at times. You'll feel lost, scared, bone-tired, and full of self-doubt. You might even cry yourself to sleep once or twice. You'll fail far more often than you succeed—and sometimes, you won't even know when you've succeeded. The code isn't for everyone. Not everyone wants to be a master and commander enough to actually become one."

After everything that had happened that day—and all the taunts from Ted—losing friends didn't seem so bad. But the seriousness in Peter's voice gave Tim pause. He thought for a moment before replying.

"I . . . want to know the code, Peter," Tim said slowly.

"Okay, fair enough. Now tell me—what are you willing to sacrifice to take charge of your course, to become a master and commander? How important is it to you, really? Is it just a nice-to-have, or is it an absolute must-have in your life?"

Before Tim could answer, the wily captain continued. "These are big questions, Tim. I don't expect you to answer tonight. Sleep on it. Really think about what it would feel like to chart your own course, to leave the safety of a familiar harbor for a land you're not even sure exists. Imagine being at sea without sight of land, knowing no one can help you. But then imagine the joy of finding a new harbor—and learning new skills to discover even more harbors. What would you do with the knowledge and courage to go anywhere and accomplish anything that truly matters to you?"

Tim's mind raced. He had never thought like this before. His heart pounded as he imagined charting his own courses around the world. Where would he go first? What improvements would he make to his boat? What about all the money he'd make—what would he spend it on? His thoughts darted from one daydream to the next until Peter gently brought him back to reality.

"Tonight, I'll share a couple of sea stories and tell you about the life I've encountered outside Hardwork Harbor. Then, if you wake up tomorrow as excited as you are right now, if you've given real thought to what you're willing to sacrifice to become a master and commander, and if you're willing to share those thoughts with me, I'll welcome you aboard the *Persistence* and teach you the code. Sound fair?"

Tim almost missed the question, staring at Peter as if truly seeing him for the first time. He couldn't believe what he was hearing. Afraid the master and commander might change his offer, Tim nodded rapidly.

As Peter smiled at Tim, Jack bounded around the counter to personally serve their chowder and fried clams. "Okay, sailors, take it slow and savor every bite. It doesn't get any better than this!" Jack beamed as he delivered two cups of piping-hot, creamy clam chowder and two heaping plates of golden-fried full-belly clams atop thinly sliced fries and coleslaw. Placing a bottle of his own branded malt vinegar between them, he said, "Enjoy, boys!"

They barely managed a quick "Thank you, Jack" before turning their full attention to tasting his creations. After a few moments of silent savoring, Peter began sharing sea stories.

Tim listened as Peter described how the *Persistence* nearly sank when it encountered ice in the Northwest Passage and how Peter spent a winter in a remote harbor with a village of Inuit. The villagers helped weld steel plates to the bow, allowing the *Persistence* to navigate the icy waters without sinking.

Then came the story of how Peter traveled to Africa to deliver food and medicine to a starving nation, only to discover there were no piers to unload the desperately needed cargo. Peter devised a way to move an anchor and motorized winch to the stern of the *Persistence*, purposely running his ship bow-first onto the beach to off-load supplies. Using his stern-powered anchor, he pulled the vessel off the shore, and because the stern was in deeper water, the propellers remained undamaged.

Peter's final story was about transporting cargo halfway around the world, a job typically reserved for the largest ships because of the fuel requirements. Working with engineers, Peter developed a battery system that recharged from the main engines, allowing him to travel farther with less fuel—and win business against larger fleets.

Tim was captivated by these stories of invention, resourcefulness, and adventure. Oh, how he longed to know what it felt like to conquer the northern seas, help a starving village, or outsmart the big ships. He was so caught up in the stories that Peter had to remind him to finish his meal—Jack wouldn't be happy if he didn't clean his plate.

As the meal ended, Tim wanted more stories, but Peter hinted he'd have to wait until tomorrow. They thanked Jack and praised him for making their food perfectly. Waving goodbye to the chef, Peter confirmed he'd meet Jack the next afternoon.

When they reached the gangway of the *Persistence*, Peter said, "Okay, Tim, you've got the helm. You decide the next course. If you're ready to tell me what you'd give up to learn the code, I'll see you soon. If not, it was a pleasure dining with you, and I wish you all the best in your career as a captain."

Tim had so many questions, but knew from Peter's tone that tonight wasn't the time. It was clear he needed to think seriously before earning more time with this remarkable captain. As Peter shook Tim's hand, he managed one last question.

"Thank you, skipper. This was a wonderful evening. And if you don't mind me asking, what do all those nicknames Jack called you mean?"

Peter released Tim's hand, smiled as he turned to the gangplank, and glanced back over his shoulder. "Persistent Pete." He gave Tim a wink, then disappeared into his quarters aboard the *Persistence*.

Tim lingered, quietly repeating the nickname. There was so much he could learn from this man that he didn't want to leave. He knew he wanted to learn the code. He wanted to shout after Persistent Pete that he'd be back tomorrow. But he also wanted Peter to know he was taking the question seriously.

A flicker of unease stirred in Tim. The captain's intensity was undeniable. Could Tim really be like him? Could he convince the master and commander to teach him the code?

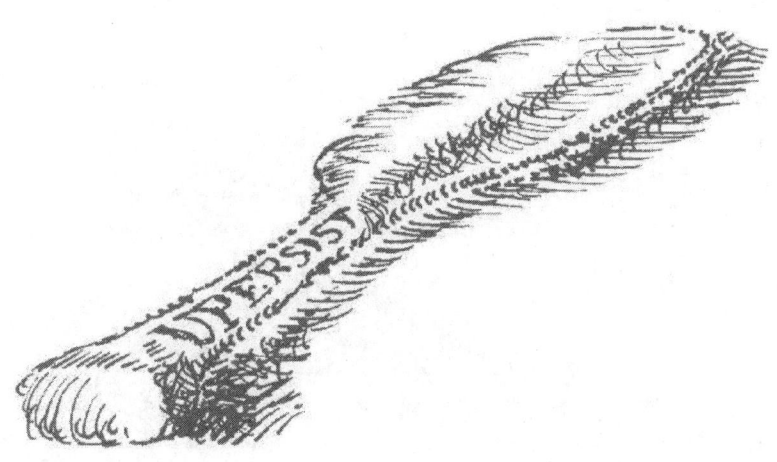

ACTION #1
Understand the Why

Tim didn't sleep well that night. He desperately wanted to come up with the perfect answer for Captain Peter so he could learn the Master and Commander Code. But all he could think of was giving up trying to hang out with Ted.

He kept repeating the question aloud: "What am I willing to give up? What will I sacrifice to learn the code?"

Then he remembered the captain's earlier remark: "Understand the 'why,' and you'll figure out the 'way.'"

Tim was stuck. He wanted to learn the code, but he wasn't sure at what cost. His thoughts shifted to what it would be like to travel the world, to help others, see new places, and learn new things. He began thinking about life in a new way—not as a balance of work and play. *What if he no longer worked to live, but lived to work? What if work wasn't just a job, but something more—with a purpose beyond a paycheck?* What if his work could make a difference in the world? What would he give up to live a life with purpose?

As the sun rose, turning the water around his boat into a golden mirror, a thought struck Tim: The captain wanted him to understand his *why*. If Tim could understand his *why*, the captain would help him discover the *way*.

Watching bubbles ripple the water's surface as the maintenance crew worked below, Tim paced his decks, thinking hard about his *why*. School had taught him how to do things correctly—but not how to do the right thing for himself. University had prepared him to follow rules, to serve in a larger organization, and to get the job done. But what the master and commander was saying felt completely different—exciting, but terrifying.

The real question wasn't whether Tim could do a job. It was whether he was willing to live his dreams.

Tim began to question himself. Did he really want the master and commander's way of life? Did he want to live with such risk? Every captain in the fleet knew that if they worked hard and delivered the goods, they'd be well paid over time and could eventually retire to cruise the coastal waterways. But Peter had left that security behind to follow his own course. Could Tim do the same?

Doubt crept in as fatigue set in. How could he navigate the high seas when he'd failed to navigate the bay just the day before?

As these thoughts swirled, Tim watched a barge pass by, pulled by a tug. He noticed the barge captain sitting at the helm, casually reading a newspaper. The captain clearly didn't care where the barge was being towed—why should he? He couldn't steer it anyway. "I guess I'd read the newspaper too, if my boat was a barge," Tim muttered.

That sparked another thought: the barge captain was working to help someone else fulfill *their* dreams. He was working because he had to, not because he wanted to. The barge captain wasn't following his own dream—unless his dream was to captain a barge. But Tim doubted that. Why would anyone want to spend their life being towed around and told what to do?

In that moment, Tim's mind shifted. He didn't want to spend his life helping other captains achieve their dreams. He wanted to chart his own course. He wanted to pursue *his* dreams—and he was willing to sacrifice everything to do it. If he only had one life to live, why not live the way he wanted?

The barge captain

With a satisfied expression, Tim saluted the barge captain, as if to say, "Thanks for helping me understand my 'why.'"

Later that day, after a quick nap, Tim paced the pier in front of the mighty *Persistence*. She glistened under the late-day sun, every inch built with purpose. Now that Tim understood the reasoning behind some of her modifications—like the double-thick bow and massive stern anchor—he admired her even more. He wondered what other upgrades the master and commander had made when he felt a strong hand squeeze his shoulder.

Startled, Tim turned to find Captain Peter in a wetsuit, dripping with salt water, a scuba tank strapped to his back. It took Tim a moment to recognize him—he hadn't expected to see Peter in diving gear.

"Ah, Captain Peter?" Tim asked, still surprised.

"The one and only, and stop calling me captain," Peter said with a wink.

Regaining his composure, Tim asked, "Are you a diver too?" It puzzled him—he'd never heard of a captain learning to scuba dive, let alone diving in the murky waters of Hardwork Harbor.

"I'm checking the work that was just done on the *Persistence*," Peter replied calmly, dropping his fins onto the pier and unstrapping his tank. "I came to swap out my propellers for these new ones I've been reading about. They create less drag and are supposed to be the next big breakthrough in propulsion. I figured they were worth testing. My attitude is, 'If you're not improving your ship, you're not improving—and when you stop improving, you start slowing down.' And I'm not ready to slow down, Tim. You tracking with me?"

Tim nodded, making a mental note to remember Peter's words. "But I still don't get the scuba gear. There are plenty of skilled divers around here—why dive yourself?" He watched as Peter laid the scuba tank next to his fins.

"A wise captain once told me, 'Trust, but verify.' I trust the propeller company to do a great job—that's why I'm here—but these propellers are critical. If they don't work, I'm dead in the water. I want to know everything about them—and more importantly, I want to learn how to fix them when something goes wrong, like hitting a sandbar." Peter smirked and gave Tim a playful poke in the ribs.

Tim forced a half-laugh at Peter's comment, glancing back at his boat where the dive crew was surfacing. He wondered if he should jump in with a mask to inspect their work.

He thought about where to find a mask—he didn't have one onboard, and he didn't know how to scuba dive—when Peter interrupted. "Well, I assume you're not here to watch me get out of my diving gear. What can I do for you, Tim?"

"I . . . I'd like to learn the code, Peter," Tim stammered. "I've thought long and hard about it."

Peter nodded slowly, giving Tim another of his laser-focused stares. "Are you ready to tell me what you're willing to give up to learn the code?"

"I am," Tim replied, straightening his back.

"Excellent!" Peter exclaimed. "Come aboard and make yourself comfortable in the wardroom. I'll be there shortly." He motioned for Tim to follow while carrying his gear to the dive locker in the *Persistence*'s stern.

Peter returned to the galley a few minutes later, but it was more than enough time for Tim's clammy hands to turn to dripping sweat as he prepared his thoughts.

When Peter entered the wardroom, he moved with the energy of someone half his age. Tim noticed how lightly Peter walked—his heels barely touched the floor, as if he were always on the balls of his feet. Tim hadn't realized before just how fit Peter was for someone thirty years his senior.

Peter grinned, waiting for Tim to speak.

Tim began slowly, marshalling his thoughts. "I've thought a lot about what you told me last night. I'm sure I want to be a master and commander. I want to help people like you do, travel the world, make improvements to my ship, and—"

Tim thought praising Peter's accomplishments would win him over, but Peter raised his hand, signaling him to stop mid-sentence.

"This isn't about doing what I've done—it's about doing what *you* want to do. It's about charting your own course and having the courage to steer it." Peter paused to let the words sink in. "Everyone wants a nice ship, great experiences, or lots of money, but not everyone is willing to *really* work for it. Not everyone understands that it's not about the harbor you land in—it's about the course you took to get there."

Peter leaned in with even more intensity than the night before. "Now, tell me, Tim—what are you willing to give up to follow your own course?"

"I . . . I'd dedicate my life to following the code."

Peter squinted at Tim, as if sighting him through a rifle scope, then leaned back slowly. "What do you mean by that?"

Tim fidgeted on the edge of his seat, rubbing his hands nervously. He glanced around the galley, took a deep breath, and let his emotions guide his answer.

"Last night, you talked about understanding the 'why'—how if I understood the why, I'd figure out the way."

"Yes, keep going," Peter encouraged.

"That got me thinking about what course I want to take in life, and how I only have one life to chart those courses—so why not chart the ones that matter most to me?"

Peter's eyes widened, and a grin spread across his face. He leaned forward, clearly excited, encouraging Tim to continue. Tim picked up on Peter's energy and began speaking with more confidence, straight from the heart.

"As I spent all night trying to figure out the right answer to your question, I realized there is no one right answer—only the right answer for me. It lies in understanding the 'why' behind why I want to learn the code to become a master and commander. And if I understand the 'why,' maybe you'll help me figure out the 'way.'"

Peter spoke slowly as he asked, "And what did you come to understand about your 'why'?"

Tim took a deep breath. "Today, I watched a captain who was given a boat just like mine years ago, but he let it become a barge. Now, he spends his days following someone else's course. I don't want that. I don't want to work just to live—I want to *live* to work. I want to be excited about the course I'm on. I want purpose. I want my life to mean something."

Peter smiled, nodding as Tim spoke. With one final deep breath, Tim concluded, "And I'm willing to spend the rest of my life following courses that inspire me. That's the kind of life worth living, and I'm ready to risk it all for it."

Peter jumped to his feet, leaping across the room, and grabbed Tim's shoulders. "That's what I'm talking about, Tim! That's what life is all about—having the courage to follow your own courses!"

Tim had to brace his core to absorb the elder captain's enthusiastic shoulder shake. Peter's strength surprised him, but more than that he felt relieved—speaking from the heart had been exactly what Peter was looking for.

Before Tim could ask, Peter grinned and said the words that made him beam. "It would be my honor to share with you the code for becoming a master and commander! But before I do," he added, "we need to discuss a few things. First, there are eight actions that define the Master and Commander Code. I say 'actions' because action is what's needed to make anything happen. I'll explain each one, but . . ."

Peter paused, allowing Tim a moment to collect himself after the whirlwind of excitement, and with a smile added: "I have one more question for you."

Tim gave a slow, cautious nod.

"Tim, do you know how to dream?"

The question caught Tim completely off guard "Huh?"

"Do you know how to dream? Because most people don't. It's nothing to be ashamed of—most folks let their minds wander to whatever catches their fancy in the moment."

Tim still wasn't following. "I thought dreaming is just what your mind does when you sleep," he said sheepishly.

"Oh yes," Peter replied, "that's one kind of dreaming. But I'm talking about training your mind to dream about what *you* want it to dream."

Tim remained bewildered. Sure, he'd daydreamed—about a bigger boat or beating Ted on a cargo route. But this wasn't what Peter meant, and Tim knew it. As he struggled to respond, Peter broke the silence.

"To become a master and commander, you first need to know how to dream. The code doesn't work without a dream to follow. And to dream big—dreams that *fire you up*—you have to learn how to dream deliberately. The bigger the dreams, the better."

Tim didn't know what to say. No one had ever asked him to dream before. The last time anyone talked to him about dreams was when his parents comforted him after a nightmare. He fidgeted in his chair, nodding but saying nothing.

"The problem is, Tim, most people don't make time to dream. They don't ask the 'what' questions. Great dreams come from great questions. The better the questions, the more exciting the dreams!" Peter said with enthusiasm.

"Ah, okay, like what kind of questions?" Tim asked, a hint of skepticism in his voice.

"I know this might sound far-fetched, but how do you think I came up with the idea to steam through the Northwest Passage, deliver supplies to that tribe in Africa, or create a fuel-saving system to cross the Pacific? I wasn't born with these ideas. I didn't come pre-programmed with these courses. I dreamed them up—and it all started with one question: *What would I do if I knew I would succeed?*"

Before Tim could respond, Peter continued. "Think about that question, Tim. I mean *really* think about it—without limitations. It's harder than it sounds because, whether you realize it or not, your brain has already accepted limits imposed by other people."

Peter pressed on. "The key to dreaming is to do it without limits, with reckless abandon, as if no one is watching or judging. Dreaming is personal—it's what makes you *you*. But to dream big dreams, you have to unlearn the rules you've absorbed from home, school, and work."

Tim's eyes began to light up, his eyebrows rising as Peter's words clicked.

"Tim, listen carefully—this is a fact to live by," Peter said as he stood from his chair, grabbed a black pen and notepad from a nearby nightstand, and handed them to Tim. Speaking slowly, he emphasized, "You have only two limitations in life." He held up one finger. "First—your imagination." Then a second finger. "Second—your determination."

Peter paused, watching Tim mouth the words to himself while frantically scribbling them on the notepad. The master and commander stiffened, his voice growing stern with conviction as he locked eyes with Tim.

"No one—and I mean *no one*—decides your limitations. You alone decide what you can or can't do. Do you understand? Don't accept a limitation unless you've proven to yourself it's real—and even then, you don't have to accept it." Peter's tone remained slow and deliberate to ensure Tim absorbed the full weight of his words. "Too many young captains accept others' limitations as their own. Just because someone says you can't do something doesn't mean you can't. *You* must decide that for yourself. One of my favorite sayings is, 'Whether you think you can, or you think you can't—you're right.'"

Peter watched as Tim whispered the phrase aloud. Feverishly, Tim jotted it down.

"You see, dreaming and limitations go hand in hand. If you believe in limitations, your dreams will shrink to fit them. You'll never allow yourself to dream bigger."

A light bulb went off in Tim's mind, and he nearly shouted, "But wait! How do I know which limitations I've accepted aren't really mine?"

Peter smiled—his student was listening. "You won't know until you start asking more questions."

"Like what?" Tim asked eagerly.

"Not 'like what,'" Peter corrected. "Ask 'what if.'"

Tim looked puzzled. "I'm not sure I follow." The layers of questions were making his head spin.

"Tim, as you dream about what you'd do if you knew you'd succeed, keep asking, 'What if?' When I dreamed of competing with the big fleets for routes halfway around the world, I got stuck on the fact that my ship's fuel tank wasn't big enough. But it was only after I asked 'What if?' that I dreamed up the idea of using batteries to extend my range."

Peter continued. "The battery idea wasn't my first. I dreamt of harnessing the wind. At first, I thought about adding sails, but that meant installing a mast, boom, and a deeper keel—too many modifications. So, I

Captain Peter

imagined using a massive kite-boarding sail without a mast. I kept refining ideas until I finally settled on developing a battery system to give me the range I needed."

Tim began to see the logic behind Peter's process and smiled, nodding slowly in agreement.

"These dreams didn't happen overnight. It took time and focus to come up with the idea—and even longer to turn it into reality."

"But you did it!" Tim exclaimed. "You invented a system that helped you beat the big guys!"

Peter smiled. "Yes, I did, but that wasn't my only reason for inventing it. Competing with the big fleets was part of it, but the real 'why' behind my effort was realizing that, without the system, I'd never get the chance to explore certain regions of the world. Once I saw that limitation, I knew I didn't want it in my life."

Tim jumped to his feet, grinning. "That was your 'why,' and the battery system was your way!"

A broad smile spread across Peter's face. Tim had caught on: the 'why' was the key—and once you understood it, the way forward became clear.

Tim beamed with excitement—he'd grasped the idea. The purpose, the 'why' behind the dream, was the starting point to chart a course of action. His mind buzzed with ideas as he imagined answering the question: *What would I do if I knew I'd succeed?*

As if on cue, Peter gently interrupted Tim's thoughts. "That's exactly right, Tim. Congratulations—you've just learned the first action to becoming a master and commander: **Understand your why, and you'll figure out the way.**"

Peter repeated the action calmly before continuing, "This is the single most important first step in making any dream come true. You have to understand why the dream matters to *you*. Dig into the 'why.' Ask yourself why you should commit your most precious resource—your time—toward pursuing it."

Tim sat down slowly, tilted his head, and asked, "What's my most precious resource?"

"Time," Peter answered, pausing for effect. "Time, Tim. Each of us only gets so much of it, and how you spend it is up to you. But once it's used, it's gone—you can't get it back. So make it count, every minute. I'm not saying don't have fun, but be aware of where your time goes. You wouldn't believe what you can accomplish by managing it well. The bigger the dream, the more time it takes to make it real."

"Got it. I'm tracking with you, Peter," Tim said, scribbling notes. "So, what's Action #2?"

Peter leaned in for emphasis. "Before we move on, you need to really understand Action #1."

Tim shot him a high-energy look. "I got it! Understand my why, and I'll figure out the way."

Peter wasn't convinced. He raised his tone slightly, driving the lesson home. "Tim, this is easy to say but hard to do. Unfortunately, you'll only understand its importance by living it. When I first left the harbor, I thought I knew my 'why.' I wanted to earn enough to repaint my ship, add shiny cleats, and upgrade the exhaust stacks. But that 'why' wasn't strong enough to keep me going when the waves turned against me."

Peter paused to let the words sink in. "I didn't even make it past the breakwater. Waves slammed my bow, and water flooded the bilges faster than the pumps could drain. I was sinking, and all I could think about was how fast I could get back to the harbor."

Tim's eyes widened in disbelief. "What did you do?"

"I panicked," Peter admitted. "I realized sinking wasn't worth a few fancy upgrades. I tried to turn back, but the waves hit me broadside, making things worse. I was going down, so I did the only thing I could: I powered up and ran my boat aground."

Tim sat frozen in shock. The thought of deliberately running a boat aground was unimaginable—but Peter had chosen it over losing his ship entirely.

While Tim absorbed the story, Peter pressed on. "I spent that night stranded, hammered by waves. I didn't sleep, lost everything not tied down—basically, everything. By the time the rescue tugs arrived at slack tide the next morning, I didn't even have a line left to throw them. I was a mess."

Tim asked quietly, "What did you do next? What happened to your boat?"

"I spent six months licking my wounds, listening to everyone in the harbor tell me how stupid my stunt was. Worse, I started believing them. I thought about settling for a life running local routes inside Hardwork Harbor. I got pretty good at convincing myself that I could climb the ranks in one of those fleets and have a decent life. I'd almost talked myself—and my friends—into believing I'd never try another 'crazy' course outside the harbor. That's when I met a master and commander, and she shared with me what I'm sharing with you now."

Peter stood and walked to the galley to get drinks, his voice steady as he recalled his near-death experience and how it almost kept him in the harbor. As he filled two glasses with ice water, he raised his voice slightly to continue. "Do you know what one of the first things that master and commander told me was? She said, 'Peter, never leave the harbor without a why worth dying for.'"

Tim's jaw dropped. "She told you that? A 'why' worth dying for?"

Peter gave a slow nod, letting the gravity of the words settle.

"Uh, Peter, I'm not looking to die anytime soon," Tim said sheepishly. "What did she really mean by that?"

Peter handed Tim a glass of water, looked him straight in the eye, and, as he sat back down, explained, "She meant you need a why you're willing to sacrifice everything for. She wasn't talking about setting a suicidal course—far from it. The point was that most people think they know their why, but they quit long before they achieve their dream."

Peter took a sip of water, preventing Tim from interjecting, and continued. "She wanted me to understand that most people don't have a strong enough reason to stay on course when things get tough. Take me, for example—I didn't even get past the breakwater before I realized that wanting shiny new hardware wasn't enough to risk sinking my ship."

Peter set down his glass and leaned forward. "This master and commander had served in the military before charting her own courses. She'd faced situations where she had to ask herself whether the mission she was ordered to steer was worth dying for. That's how she came to define a true why—one that's worth everything."

Peter paused, studying Tim's body language to ensure his words were sinking in. "It's an interesting question, one I've asked myself many times: What do I feel so strongly about that I'd be willing to die trying to accomplish it?"

"I've never thought of asking myself that," Tim mumbled, staring down at his notes, uneasy about even saying the word "die."

Noticing Tim's discomfort, Peter responded in a reassuring tone. "Relax, Tim. No one's asking you to die for your 'why.' I just want you to find a 'why' strong enough to keep you going when things get tough. And trust me, they *will* get tough. That's when you'll need to ask yourself the next question."

Tim sat up slightly, sensing some relief. "What question is that?"

"When waves crash over your bow, winds blow you off course, currents drag you backward, and you haven't slept in days, you'll ask yourself, 'Is this course worth steering? Is all the struggle really worth it?' At first, it'll be a fleeting thought, but as the course gets harder, doubt will creep in. It'll try to convince you to turn around and head to a safe harbor—one that promises shelter from the storm."

Tim nodded, wide-eyed, trying to imagine the harrowing scene Peter described.

"When that doubt knocks, you need to be ready to knock it back. And the best way to do that is by understanding your 'why.' You with me, Tim?"

"Oh, I'm with you, Peter," Tim replied, jotting a quick note: **Beat doubt back by building stronger whys.**

"Good," Peter said firmly. "Because I can't stress this enough: Don't ever go to sea without knowing your 'why.' I've seen good captains sink because they sailed for the wrong reasons. And the saddest part? They had what it took to become masters and commanders, but they didn't understand their 'why.' If they had, they would have discovered Action #2."

Tim sat bolt upright, excitement bubbling over. "What's that—what's Action #2?"

Peter responded with a single word: "Plan."

HOW TO
GET STARTED

ACTION #1 | UNDERSTAND YOUR *WHY*

All these years later, I can still hear the pulmonary doctor's words as if it were yesterday: "Mrs. Mills, I recommend that your son learn the game of chess."

Those aren't words most twelve-year-olds want to hear—especially one who loved hunting snakes, frogs, and turtles, riding his bike, and exploring the outdoors. My eyes filled with tears as I tried to imagine giving up all that. Thankfully, my mom sent me out of the room before the doctor could finish explaining how severe my asthma was. I sat in the waiting room, crying quietly. The more I thought about everything I'd never do again, the more I cried.

Once again, Mom came to my rescue. When she found me crying, she dug her fingernails into my forearm and said, "Alden, look at me and remember these words: No one—and I mean NO ONE—decides what you can or can't do. You decide—no one else."

In that moment, my mom taught me the essence of Action #1: Understand what you want to do, then do it. That day, she set me on a new course—one that would include overcoming asthma, leading U.S. Navy SEALs, and building companies. At twelve, I couldn't fully grasp the lesson she was teaching: my life was up to me—not the asthma doctor, not a teacher, not a classmate, but me. It's a simple concept: Each of us decides what we can or can't do. No one else makes that decision.

It gets harder, however, when you're chasing a dream you're not sure you can achieve—which is true of most dreams worth pursuing. When I decided to become a Navy SEAL, I compiled a list of reasons why making it through training was crucial. Yet even with those reasons, I struggled with internal doubts—not to mention the doubts the SEAL instructors were quick to sow. Those doubts returned years later when I was starting the Perfect Fitness Company. This time, the SEAL instructors were replaced by impatient investors questioning why I wouldn't give up and get a "real job." Six months before we launched the Perfect Pushup, one investor told me, "Alden, it's over. You're starting to embarrass yourself."

Conquering asthma, becoming a SEAL, and launching a company were personal goals. Though different, each required the same fundamental steps: They all started with a clear understanding of what I wanted to accomplish—and, more importantly, why.

Here are a few examples:

- **Conquering asthma:** The idea of not being able to go outside, play with friends, explore the woods, and ride my bike was intolerable. I decided I'd rather be sick for life than give up the things that made me happy.
- **Becoming a Navy SEAL:** As a Naval Academy graduate, I had committed to five years of service. I loved the water, team sports, and being outdoors, but the thought of spending five years in a submarine or engine room was horrifying. I was willing to suffer heavily to avoid that confinement. (Ironically, I later led two mini-sub SEAL

platoons and spent months on submarines, only to find it wasn't as bad as I imagined.)
- **Launching a company:** I couldn't see myself climbing a corporate ladder with someone else dictating my pay and vacation time. I also wanted to look my kids in the eyes and tell them they could do anything they set their minds to—and how could I say that without proving it myself?

These examples are what I call **Milestone Goals**—major accomplishments that took years to achieve and became life-changing milestones. You reach Milestone Goals by completing **Pebble Goals** along the way. For example, to get into SEAL training, I had to do 120 push-ups, 100 sit-ups, and 20 pull-ups, plus a 1.5-mile run and an 800-yard swim. None of these came easily; each became a Pebble Goal.

Intermediate goals are essential to success, but the key is learning not to give up on your way to the ultimate destination—the Milestone Goal. **How do you build unstoppable persistence?** It starts with understanding your **"why"**—your reason for pursuing the goal. Knowing your why is the fuel that keeps you going when others tell you to quit. It helps you push back the inevitable doubts that will creep into your mind. Your why is the engine that drives perseverance, even when you think you can't keep going. **It's that important. Know your why before you start!**

So how do you figure out your why? What works for me is using what I call **Outcome Accounts.** Whenever I come up with a new Milestone Goal, I create an Outcome Account. It's a simple way to test how important the goal really is. Some goals are just nice-to-haves, while others are must-haves. Outcome Accounts help me identify which goals truly matter, especially for those that require months or even years of persistence to achieve.

Here's how an Outcome Account works:

- **At the top of a sheet of paper**, write and underline your goal. Example: *I want to graduate from the Naval Academy.*
- **Divide the paper in half** with a vertical line.

- **Label the left column** with a plus sign (+) and the right with a minus sign (-).
- **In the plus column**, list every positive outcome of achieving the goal. For example:
  — I would be the first in my family to achieve this.
  — I could serve as a naval officer.
  — I would have a shot at becoming a Navy SEAL platoon commander.
  — I'd do things few people get to do.
  — I'd prove wrong the people who said I couldn't make it—including a few teachers and officers.
- **In the minus column**, list every negative outcome of not achieving it. For example:
  — I'd have to serve in the Navy as an enlisted sailor to repay my time at the Academy.
  — Everyone who doubted me would say, "I told you so."
  — It would take me much longer to earn a commission or become a SEAL commander.
  — I'd feel I failed at something I believed I could do.
  — I'd let myself down by not trying hard enough and choosing the easy way out.

These pluses and minuses clarified why I needed to stay at the Academy and graduate. At the end of my sophomore year, I considered leaving, but I found motivation in both columns: the rewards of graduating and the consequences of quitting. Both fueled my determination when people insisted I couldn't do it. By the end of my sophomore year, I had racked up the maximum demerits for a senior. To graduate, I needed to avoid getting another demerit for two whole years! My company officer even told me I'd never make it.

But I did. And I did so by using many of the reasons listed in my Outcome Account. Freud's theory of human behavior—*avoiding pain and seeking pleasure*—applied perfectly. My biggest motivator wasn't just the positive outcomes; it was avoiding the satisfaction my doubters would feel if I failed. That became my primary driver to persevere through those final two years.

Over time, I began creating Outcome Accounts mentally. I'd go through the pluses and minuses in my mind until I found one that hit me in the gut and sparked a daydream of success. At the Academy, I would fall asleep imagining the faces and voices of my doubters. I visualized every detail of what graduation day would feel like, knowing that if I ever saw those doubters again, I'd prove them wrong. I didn't realize it at the time, but I was personalizing my goal and reinforcing it through visualization. The more I did this, the more determined I became to see it through.

For every significant goal I've pursued since, I've relied on an Outcome Account to define my reason for working hard, staying focused, and filtering out those who help from those who hinder. The Outcome Account remains my most important first step toward being **UNSTOPPABLE**. As Master and Commander Peter teaches Captain Tim: **"Once you understand your why, you'll figure out your way."**

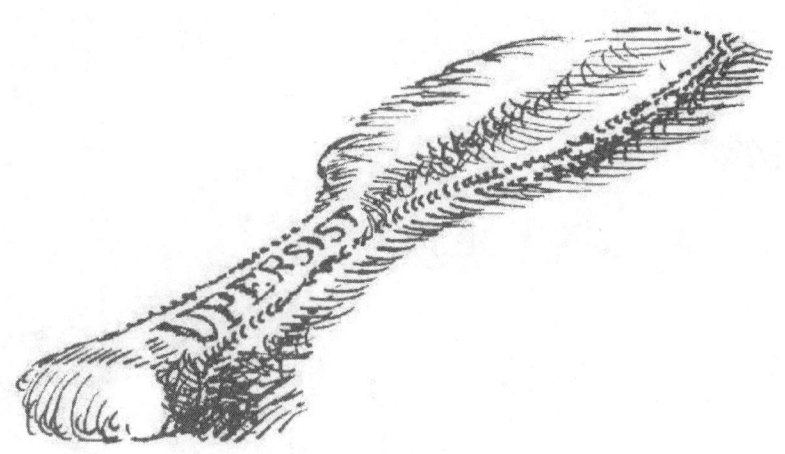

ACTION #2
Plan in 3-D

Tim sat across from the seasoned captain, confusion written across his face. "Action #2 is to plan? That's it?"

"Yep. First you understand, then you plan," Peter said with a grin.

"Okay. Understand, then plan. What's Action #3?" Tim asked, hoping the next action would be more exciting than planning.

Peter's grin grew wider. "I'll tell you Action #3 after you explain the plan you made to cross the bay yesterday."

Tim squirmed a bit, struggling to recall a course he had been trying to forget for the past day. "Uh, well . . . I didn't really write it down. I

just followed my usual route until I reached buoy #7 and turned to course zero-one-zero."

Peter leaned in slightly, his eyes twinkling with curiosity. "So, you didn't write down the new course. Why not?"

Tim exhaled in resignation. "I didn't think it was that important. I mean, I knew part of the route from sailing it all year. I didn't expect the new leg to be that hard." His shoulders slumped, the weight of his mistake settling in.

Peter was quick to respond, cutting through Tim's self-doubt. "Of course you didn't—any young captain would've done the same thing. I did exactly that when I was your age. I was so excited about heading to a new town that I spent ten seconds thinking about the course before casting off. All I could imagine was the night life on the other side of the bay. I was daydreaming right up until my engine died in the middle of the channel."

Tim's eyes widened. "Wait . . . your engine died on your very first trip across the bay?"

Peter leaned back, hands clasped behind his head, a broad, toothy smile spreading across his face. "Yep, ran out of diesel fuel! Smack in the middle of the bay at the busiest time of the day, with a line of big ships barreling down behind me. I almost got run over! Had to swerve out of the channel and ended up drifting onto a sandbar. And since the bay was so crowded, the tow fleet couldn't get to me until the day's end."

Tim stared in shock. Peter's laughter filled the room, leaving Tim even more bewildered. How could Peter be laughing about such a disaster?

Ran out of gas

"Am I missing something? I don't see what's so funny," Tim said, his voice edged with frustration.

Peter wiped a tear from his eye, still chuckling. "Oh, Tim, nothing was funny about it *then*. I was mortified—I didn't want to show my face on a pier for years!"

Tim shook his head, unconvinced. "So, why laugh now? I ran aground just yesterday, and the last thing I want to do is tell anyone about it, let alone laugh."

Peter leaned forward, tone softening. "I felt exactly like you do when it happened. I took it personally. I sulked for weeks, avoided every captain I knew, and my friends teased me at every opportunity. It was the worst experience of my early career."

Tim still looked skeptical, but Peter gave him a knowing smile. "I laugh now because it's not a failure anymore—it's a lesson learned."

Tim's frown deepened, and Peter continued gently. "Look, Tim, I've failed far more times than I've succeeded. But here's the thing: I treat failure not as a setback but as a step forward. Every failure teaches me what doesn't work—and that's just as valuable as knowing what does. If you want to be a master and commander, you need to embrace failure as a positive, not a negative."

Peter's voice softened. "The grand master and commander who taught me the code would say, 'The only real mistake is the one from which we learn nothing.'"

Tim squirmed in his chair, imagining a future where he might laugh about running his boat aground. "Okay, I get what your master and commander told you, but this goes against everything we learned at Uptoyou University. You don't get ahead by making mistakes on exams, and you definitely don't laugh about them afterward. So why would I need to fail in order to learn new things?"

Peter sat up, took a slow sip of water, and nodded patiently. "I didn't say you *should* fail to learn new things. I said, '*When* you fail, learn from it.' There's a big difference. Failing is just part of the learning process. The sooner you embrace that, the better a captain you'll become."

Tim let out a small sigh of relief. He had begun to wonder if Peter was suggesting he throw away everything he'd learned in school.

"And you're right," Peter continued. "Exams aren't the place to make mistakes. But homework? That's exactly where mistakes are supposed to happen."

Tim's brow unfurrowed, comforted by Peter's words. The old captain leaned in, his tone sharpening as he laid the foundation for Tim's next lesson. "Listen carefully, Tim. Before you leave a safe harbor, there are three things to know."

Peter slowed his pace and lowered his voice, adding weight to each word. Raising his right hand, he counted them off: "#1: *The Why*—Why is this new course important to you? #2: *The What*—What's the destination? And #3: *The How*—How are you going to get there?"

Tim scrambled to jot down the points, but Peter wasn't finished. "Captain Tim, eyes on me!" Peter's voice was sharp but not unkind. "This isn't complicated. You'll have plenty of time to take notes. I want you to *understand* this—commit it to memory."

Tim set his notepad aside as Peter leaned closer, repeating the essentials slowly and deliberately. "Say them with me: Why, What, and How." Together, they echoed the words aloud, their voices in sync.

Peter's tone remained serious as he drove his point home. "You must always answer these three questions before setting off on a new course. The first two—*Why* and *What*—are easy. But the *How*? That's where it gets tricky. And answering that question is what the rest of the Master and Commander Code is all about."

Peter paused, letting his words sink in. Then he asked, "How many of those Uptoyou exams did you ace?"

Tim dropped his chin slightly, mumbling, "Ah, not one."

"I know that feeling," Peter said encouragingly. "But how many times did you go back and try to understand why you missed those questions?"

"I . . . I didn't do that often. I was just relieved to get the exam over with," Tim admitted.

"Same here!" Peter nearly shouted. "Tim, when you're following your own course, it's like a final exam every day—except there's no teacher to tell you what you got wrong. You have to figure it out yourself. And the only way to know what works is to have a plan. I didn't have one the day I ran out of fuel, or when I tried to leave the harbor. But now I do, and it gives me a system to tackle new courses with confidence."

"Okay, I think I get it, but your plan sounds different from the ones they taught us in school. There, it was about planning our day or studying for a test. What's different about your method?"

"Great question!" Peter almost jumped from his seat, pointing his finger at Tim's chest. "The planning I'm talking about is called '3-D planning.'"

"Huh?" Tim said, bewildered.

"Three-dimensional planning," Peter explained. "School is great for learning concepts. They teach linear thinking: To get to C from A, you first go through B. But at sea, nothing is linear. You have to think three-dimensionally all the time—keeping track of the wind, water, waves, weather, and things like engine speed, course, depth, ship speed, and your navigation and communication gear."

Tim nodded. He understood the concepts well enough.

"A linear plan won't help you out there," Peter continued. "It didn't help either of us when we first tried crossing the bay! When you plan your course you need to do it three-dimensionally and think through the top three things that could go wrong—and have contingency plans. Some captains call this 'out-of-the-box' thinking, but I prefer calling it 3-D planning. Think of it as viewing a plan from three angles. And guess what?"

"What?" Tim asked, looking perplexed.

"Not 'what,' Tim," Peter said with a smirk. "How! When you create a plan, you're figuring out *how* to get what you want!"

Tim sat up, eyes wide. "So, the plan is the outline of 'The How'?"

"Affirmative, Captain!" Peter smiled, saluting from his chair. "And here's the best part: Even with all that planning, you'll still miss something—and *that's* when it gets exciting!"

"I don't follow," Tim said. "What's exciting about a flawed plan?"

Peter jumped to his feet. "Tim, that's the moment when you learn something new! That's why it's exciting! You use all your knowledge to think three-dimensionally, put together the best plan—and still discover you missed something. But that discovery makes you smarter and enables you to do something new. Now *that's* exciting!"

Tim couldn't help but get fired up, even though the idea of learning at sea still scared him. "I get it!" Tim shouted. "That's why you said failure is a way to learn—it makes you smarter and helps you become a better captain."

"Exactly!"

Just then, a thought hit Tim, and Peter saw the energy drain from him almost as quickly as it had sparked.

"But, Peter, if no plan is perfect, then why bother planning at all?" Tim asked.

Peter beamed—Tim was catching on.

"Excellent question! I'm glad you asked," Peter said warmly, encouraging Tim to keep his curiosity flowing. "You plan to prepare yourself for the unexpected. A grand old master and commander I know has a brass plaque mounted above his compass with these words: 'Luck favors the prepared.'"

Peter paused, waiting for Tim to jot the phrase in his notepad. "To prepare, you must first plan. The better your plan, the better you can prepare—and the better prepared you are, the greater your chances of success."

Tim scribbled the words down while Peter waited patiently. Then Peter added, "Some masters and commanders put it differently—more negatively." As Tim looked up, Peter lowered his voice. "They say, 'Failure to plan is planning for failure.'" The wily skipper leaned back in his chair, watching the words settle into Tim's thoughts.

"So there you have it, Tim—two ways to look at Action #2: the glass half-full or half-empty. I prefer the half-full approach. *Luck favors the prepared.*"

Peter smiled, seeing Tim grasp the lesson. Tim returned to his notes, writing:

ACTION #2: PLAN IN 3-D

Think about three angles of the plan—not just *where* I want to go, but *HOW* I'll get there. Consider what might change my course, and plan *HOW* to handle it.

Tim underlined *HOW* multiple times, reinforcing the message in his mind.

Peter, pleased with Tim's enthusiasm, saw a bit of himself in the younger man. Smiling, he picked up a small brass bell from the cocktail table and gave it three short rings.

Within seconds, an older gentleman in a crisp white uniform appeared, speaking with a distinct accent. "Sir, may I be of service?"

Peter nodded appreciatively. "Jacques, my colleague will join me for dinner this evening." He glanced at Tim for approval, and Tim gave a quick nod.

Peter added, "Please prepare a dinner of local seafood. Surprise us with your selections, Jacques."

The chef gave a slight bow. "It will be my pleasure, sir. Dinner will be served at 1800 hours." With that, he returned to the galley.

Peter checked his chronometer. "Perfect. We have just enough time to cover the next two actions."

HOW TO
GET STARTED

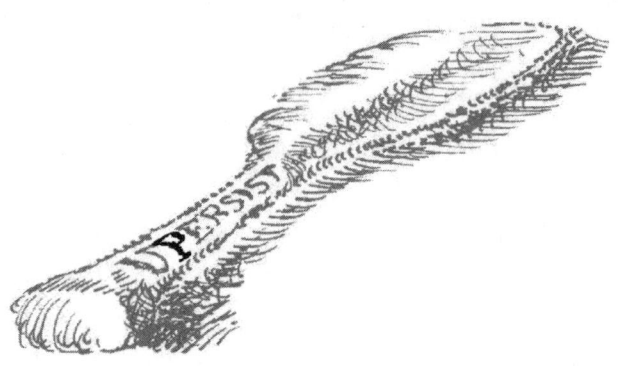

ACTION #2 | PLAN IN 3-D

"Wanna know the biggest question y'all need to answer when it comes to making it through Navy SEAL training? How much are you willing to 'pay' for it?"

We called him "Instructor Half-Butt"—though never to his face! He'd lost his left butt cheek to a rocket-propelled grenade in Vietnam. He spoke with a deep Southern drawl, delivering one-liners that perfectly summed up any situation. "I don't care how many push-ups you can crank out or how many bull's-eyes you hit—if you can't plan a mission, you've got no business leading one. Failure to plan is planning for failure, and that means your SEAL career will be a short one."

He had our undivided attention. He was leading a pilot program to prepare junior officers for platoon commander roles, taught by seasoned officers and enlisted leaders from within the SEAL community. One of the course's main goals was to instill the habit of planning—whether for missions or any other objective.

I call Action #2 "Plan in 3-D" for two reasons: it answers both the "What" and the "How."

REASON #1: THE "WHAT"

Planning requires thinking three-dimensionally—a plan is only as good as your preparation for what could go wrong. The better prepared you are, the better your chances of success.

REASON #2: THE "HOW"

Goals are achieved through action—consistent, daily action. The three essential steps are the "3 Ds":

1. **Define** the goal
2. **Divide** the goal into manageable parts
3. **Do** it daily

Whether you're leading SEALs, starting a business, or writing a book, the key is daily action. It's not enough to define your goal and understand your "why"—none of it matters without consistent follow-through. The difference between success and failure comes down to one thing: action. My goal for you is to build the habit of taking action toward your goal every day.

Planning isn't just about making lists; it's about creating the right mindset. The planning process prepares you mentally for the sacrifices and steps needed to turn your dream—your Milestone Goal—into reality. It helps you visualize the path and gets you in the right frame of mind to pursue it.

But remember, planning is just one step in your journey to success—it's not the destination. Beware of "planning paralysis," where you become so focused on perfecting the plan that you never act on it. Your plan is only as good as the actions you take.

In the SEAL teams, we had two plans: the one we made before the mission and the one we carried out during it. Never forget—the mission is to achieve your goal, not to create a perfect plan for it.

Step One: Define It

Planning isn't complicated—the real challenge is deciding what you want and what you're willing to sacrifice to get it. The key is to connect your goal with both passion and purpose. It doesn't matter which comes first, but you need both to stay inspired.

For example, I'm passionate about teamwork, adventure, boats, and guns, which made becoming a SEAL an exciting career path. But those passions alone weren't enough during training—like when I was so cold I vomited, or when I had to drill my toenails to relieve the pressure from standing for 72 hours straight. At those moments, I needed a deeper purpose to keep me going. I thought long and hard about *why* I wanted to be a SEAL, and that mindset is what carried me through.

I wasn't the fastest runner or swimmer, nor the strongest at push-ups or pull-ups. But I made up for it with determination. I watched my BUD/S (Basic Underwater Demolition/SEAL training) class shrink from 122 candidates to just 18 in the first six weeks. The men who survived Hellweek in December 1991 didn't do it because they had the biggest biceps—it came down to how deeply they believed in their reason for being there. The ones who made it wanted it more than the other 104 who didn't.

No SEAL goes on a mission without knowing its objective. The same goes for any goal: Know what you want, *why* you want it, and what you're willing to give up to achieve it. Passion will lead you to a goal worth pursuing, but purpose is what keeps you moving forward. Whether your goal is to become a SEAL, start a business, or lose thirty pounds (all goals I've pursued), you need to define your purpose, ignite your passion, and take action.

Step Two: Divide It

As BUD/S Class 181 was preparing for Hellweek, two curious classmates who also happened to be roommates managed to find a copy of the Hellweek schedule. It listed tasks we hadn't been trained to do and allowed only three and a half hours of sleep for the entire week, running from Sunday evening to Friday afternoon. These two classmates shared the schedule with others, but most of us declined, including me.

Guess what happened? Those two couldn't stop thinking about the schedule. It was so overwhelming that they started doubting themselves—and quit 24 hours before Hellweek even began. (I suspect the instructors left the schedule out on purpose, hoping to psych out anyone they could!)

The lesson? Stay focused on the moment—the task at hand, not the mountain of work ahead. No one gets through Hellweek in a single day, and no one accomplishes a big goal all at once. People often ask me, "How did you make it through SEAL training?" My answer is always the same: Focus on the next task, the next breath. (I save the deeper conversation about defining purpose for those seriously considering SEAL training.)

This is the essence of Step Two: **Divide your plan into bite-sized goals.** If you want to lose thirty pounds, you won't do it in a day, a week, or even a month. You'll do it by watching what you eat and working out every day. Whether your goal is to lose weight, start a business, or finish SEAL training, the planning approach is the same—break it down into daily or even hourly tasks. (During Hellweek, I was counting seconds!)

If your goal feels too big to make meaningful progress in a day, it means the goal needs to be divided further. One day at a time—that's how you achieve anything.

Step Three: Do It Daily

As I mentioned earlier, no plan is perfect. The only plan that matters is the one you act on. Through action, you'll discover what was missing. If your actions result in failure, embrace it—you just learned something. The only real failure is the one you don't learn from.

Thomas Edison once said, "I learned 10,000 ways not to invent the light bulb." He treated failure as a learning tool, and that's exactly the mindset to adopt when pursuing a new goal. In the SEALs, we say, "If you're not failing, you're not trying hard enough."

When people ask me how I launched Perfect Pushup, I tell them we learned $1,475,000 worth of ways *not* to launch my first product, BodyRev. (We raised $1.5 million and had just $25,000 left when Perfect Pushup launched.) Despite being on the brink of bankruptcy, we stayed determined. After we launched Perfect Pushup, *Inc.* magazine named our company the fastest-growing consumer-products company in the country in 2009—a far cry from two years earlier, when we were nearly out of business.

Whether you're starting a company or reporting for SEAL training, daily progress is the key to success. Goals are marathons, not sprints. Some days, it will feel like you've made no progress—or even lost ground. That's okay—it's part of the journey.

To stay on track, review your progress regularly. In the SEALs, we do this through a Debrief after every mission—analyzing what worked and what didn't. Use the same mindset for your goals: focus on progress, not how far you have left to go. Dwelling on the remaining distance is self-defeating. The best way to keep moving forward is to work on your goal every day.

Over time, "do it daily" will become a habit, and you'll find yourself asking each morning, *What can I do today to move closer to my goal?* This step is critical to becoming unstoppable and succeeding at anything.

Here's a simple tool I use to stay focused: "Daily Action Cards." You can make your own or find Be Unstoppable versions at www.BeUnstoppable.com. Just remember—the path to your goal is paved with daily action!

UNSTOPPABLE Daily Action Notecards
INSTRUCTIONS

Step 1 Fill out your daily action card the night before

Step 2 Commit to completing your GOALS first
(if you get stuck on a goal, take a break and complete a task)

Step 3 Take notes of lessons learned, actions and attitudes.

SAVE YOUR NOTE CARDS – they represent progress and progress is fuel for forward momentum toward achieving goals!

NOTE: IF you cannot complete a goal in a day then divide it into smaller goals until you can complete a portion of your goal in a day.

BEUNSTOPPABLE.com

ACTION #3
Exercise to Execute

"Are you ready, Tim?" Peter asked.

Tim could barely contain his excitement—he wasn't sure if he was more eager to hear Peter's wisdom or dive into the remarkable meal he was anticipating.

"Standing by to receive, Cap'n!" Tim replied with a grin.

"Good. Let's start with the importance of preparation."

Tim jumped in, "The better the plan, the better I can prepare, which makes my chances of success infinitely better."

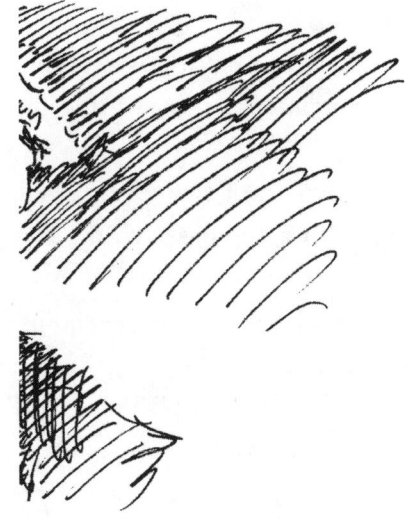

"Exactly!" Peter exclaimed. "Now, here's a question: Do you know the number one limiting factor in your ability to properly prepare and execute a plan?"

Tim winced, bracing for another tricky question. "Uh . . . my ability to stay focused?" he guessed. It felt like a long shot, but at least it was better than some of his earlier attempts.

Peter smiled. "That's actually a close second. Staying focused and avoiding distractions is definitely important. But the *number one* factor in turning a plan into reality is your ability to *do the work*."

Tim gave Peter a puzzled look and slowly repeated, "Ohhkay . . . my ability to do the work. So, is *that* Action #3?"

"It's the first part of it," Peter said, as if guiding Tim through a tricky math problem. "Action #3 has two parts. The second part can be done without the first—but you won't be nearly as effective if you skip the first."

Now Tim was confused. He'd never been good at word problems, let alone riddles. He wished Peter would just give him the answer. But the older captain seemed to enjoy making the young skipper think, and his next question caught Tim completely off guard.

"Do you know how your body works?" Peter asked, his tone curious.

Tim blinked, thrown off course, and responded cautiously, "Do you mean . . . how my ship works?"

"No, I mean your body—the one with two arms, two legs, a head, and a heart," Peter said, tilting his head with a smile, watching Tim squirm in his chair.

"Uh, well, yeah, of course I do," Tim said, hesitating. Then, squinting suspiciously, he added, "Is this a trick question, Peter?"

Peter smiled. "No, just an important one. Most people don't truly understand or appreciate how and why their body works."

It was the second time that evening Peter had made Tim uncomfortable. What did pursuing dreams have to do with the human body? But Tim quickly composed himself and leaned in, ready to listen.

"Your body is designed to do one thing and one thing only. Do you know what that is?"

Tim squirmed again and answered hesitantly, "To live?"

Peter gave a soft, encouraging response. "That's the end result, but not quite the answer I'm looking for."

Tim grimaced, and stared at the ceiling as if hoping inspiration might appear. Peter could see Tim was stuck, so he offered a hint.

"What's the one body part that modern science hasn't been able to transplant into another body?"

Tim started naming vital organs under his breath. Then suddenly sat bolt upright and blurted out, "The brain! The brain is the only organ that can't be transplanted!"

"Exactly!" Peter beamed. "Now, what is your body designed to do with the brain?"

"Uh, protect it?"

"Yes, your body protects your brain, and it also. . . ?" Peter paused, hoping Tim would complete the thought.

Tim gave him a blank stare.

"It *also obeys* your brain," Peter said. "Every action you take is within your control. We'll explore this more with the fifth action, but for now, remember: *Your body obeys your brain.*"

Peter was passionate about the connection between the body and brain. It frustrated him to see a generation of captains finishing school with poor physical conditioning. He often remarked to Jacques, the *Persistence*'s chef: "No wonder there aren't more captains leaving the harbor; they lack the stamina and strength for the long hours needed to cross an ocean. And they probably lack the confidence to try."

Peter believed that feeling good physically built the confidence needed to take on new challenges—and exercise was one of the best ways to feel good. Now he aimed to drive that point home.

"Your body feeds and protects your brain. Every system in your body is designed to support it. Your cardiovascular system pumps oxygenated blood and nutrients to your brain. Your neurological system creates pathways that allow your brain to issue commands to your muscular and skeletal systems, which produce motion. And motion means work."

Peter let the words linger, watching Tim's eyes brighten as he connected the dots between the body and brain.

Posture

"The reason I'm focusing on this fundamental, Tim, is that most people neglect their body, even though it's one of the most important assets for turning dreams into reality."

Tim nodded slowly, following Peter's line of thought.

"Your brain is the command center—it decides whether you can or can't do something. But it depends entirely on the input it receives from your body. Feed your body poorly, and your brain slows down, making decisions harder. The same thing happens if you don't exercise."

Peter jumped to his feet, exaggerating poor posture and a protruding belly. "Your body's condition directly affects your stamina—and you'll need plenty of that when setting off on a new course."

Peter paced in front of Tim, emphasizing the importance of exercise and a healthy diet when pursuing big dreams. "Did you know exercise combats around fifty ailments, from diabetes to depression?" he asked. "Exercise, healthy food, and sleep are your best medicine. Exercise builds stamina—and that's exactly what you'll need when you're at sea alone for long stretches."

Peter didn't pause long enough for Tim to respond. "And do you know what else you'll need at sea, especially when doubt creeps in and you're questioning if you're still on the right course? A positive attitude! You'll need a healthy dose of can-do spirit. And guess what happens when you exercise?"

Tim's eyes widened as Peter stomped about, radiating energy.

"Exercise fires up the can-do chemicals in your body—the same ones that combat depression," Peter continued. "It's your best defense against giving up. Are you tracking with me?"

It all clicked for Tim. He had wondered how this older captain carried his diving gear so effortlessly or how he maintained such a firm handshake and boundless energy. Now it was clear—this man was stronger and fitter than Tim had realized.

Tim smiled, catching on. "I'm tracking with you, Peter. I get it!"

Peter took a deep breath. He was living proof that exercise kept a captain young, inspired, and brimming with positive energy.

"So, what does exercise have to do with Action #3, you ask?" Peter didn't wait for Tim's reply. "Exercise strengthens the body, and the stronger your body, the more endurance you have. The more endurance you have, the more effectively you can execute your plan. Make sense?"

Peter locked eyes with Tim, his focus sharp. "It's all about execution, and exercise helps. I'll take anything that makes me better at executing. Execution is everything when you leave the harbor and chase your big, scary dream."

With that, the commander sank into his chair, taking a few deep breaths.

"So, is exercise part one of Action #3?" Tim asked, eager to get the action on paper and keep Peter on track.

"It is," Peter confirmed. "It's the first part of the third action, and if you haven't noticed by now, I think it's critical," he added with a wink.

"Oh, I get your point loud and clear, skipper," Tim said, returning the wink. "So, what's the other part?"

"The other part," Peter said matter-of-factly, "is to execute daily. Chasing a dream takes time, stamina, and momentum. Life is full of distractions, and it's easy to drift off course. You need to build a habit of executing your plan *every single day*." Peter emphasized the last words slowly and deliberately. "A plan is only a plan until you turn it into action. And exercise keeps you moving forward when you feel like giving up. I consider exercise part of executing my plan—it's the first thing I do every morning. It fires up my engine for the day and helps me stay focused as I tackle the details of executing my plans."

Tim smiled, starting to understand what made Peter such a strong captain. He felt inspired by the master and commander's energy, strength, and stamina. The more Tim listened, the more he realized he wanted to follow a similar path. If exercise gave Peter these qualities, Tim wanted to make it part of his life too.

"So, what do you call Action #3, Peter?" Tim asked. "I understand how exercise helps you execute, and I get that I need to build a daily habit of following through on my plan. But how do you define the action?"

"Oh, that's simple," Peter said. "I call it 'Exercise to Execute Daily.'" Pride filled his voice as he added, "Trust me on this, Tim. If you decide to follow the code, promise me you won't skip the exercise part. I can't tell you how many times it's saved me—both mentally and physically. There's no way I could've crossed the great blue seas without the stamina exercise gave me. It kept me on watch for hours and gave me the endurance to work day and night with the Inuit, welding steel plates onto my ship's hull so we could escape the ice floes in the Northwest Passage." Peter gave a shiver at the memory. "Exercise has saved my ship—and my life."

Peter leaned in, his voice low and serious. "When you're stuck—really stuck—and feel like quitting, take a one-hour break and get your heart pumping. Do any exercise you enjoy—I use the rowing machine—and then come back to the problem. I promise you'll have a fresh outlook and a clear mind, ready to solve whatever's in front of you. It works every time."

Tim nodded, scribbling in his notepad. He wrote the phrase with emphasis: **Exercise to Execute Daily!** He traced over the word "exercise" three times, imagining the exercises he'd commit to doing.

Just then, an intoxicating scent floated past, disrupting Tim's train of thought.

The fresh aroma had a similar effect on Peter, who broke the silence with a grin. "I believe Jacques is preparing one of my favorites—pan-seared ahi tuna. We're in for a rare treat tonight!"

The younger captain was just as eager as Peter to taste the meal but wanted to keep his mentor talking, squeezing every possible insight from their time together. Tim wished he could slow this magical evening down, though he knew that time, like the tides, waits for no one. Breaking the silence, he returned to the topic that had animated the master and commander minutes earlier.

"Peter, this all makes so much sense now. I understand the connection between exercise and my brain—I'd never thought of it that way. I also see how being in shape helps me execute a plan. I promise to make exercise part of my daily routine. But I have one question: What do you do when you don't have time to exercise?"

Peter laughed heartily. "No one *has* time to exercise unless they make it a priority!" he said. Then, without warning, he stood up, pushed the coffee table aside, and dropped to the floor, cranking out push-ups.

Push-ups

At the top of his fifth push-up, Peter turned to Tim with a grin. "Well, what are you waiting for?"

"You want me to do push-ups . . . with you?" Tim asked, startled.

"Absolutely! The best way to understand something is to experience it. Drop down and get your blood pumping," Peter commanded with a playful smirk.

Feeling a little intimidated by the older captain's energy, Tim reluctantly got on the floor. Together, they knocked out ten push-ups, though Tim's face flushed red as he struggled through the last two. His arms shook, but Peter kept encouraging him. The elder captain could've easily done another thirty but stopped at ten to keep Tim motivated, not defeated.

As Tim caught his breath, Peter gave him a hearty slap on the back. "Now that you know how to do a push-up, you'll never have an excuse not to exercise!" Peter returned to his chair, looking as relaxed as if nothing had happened.

Tim took a moment longer to collect himself. He hadn't done push-ups since high school and marveled at how effortlessly Peter had completed his set.

Peter leaned forward with some advice. "Push-ups are the best go-to exercise when you don't have time for a row or run. They engage all the major muscle groups, and you can do them anytime, anywhere. I even use them to stay awake on late-night watch or when I need a boost after a heavy lunch."

Tim wiped a bead of sweat from his temple and slid back into his chair, jotting down a mental note to start incorporating push-ups into his routine. "Point taken, skipper."

Peter grinned. "No need to stress. Push-ups have an easy learning curve. Start with sets of three to five reps throughout the day, and soon enough, you'll be knocking them out with ease. I make it fun—sometimes I do ten push-ups every time I grab a glass of water or head to the bathroom. If I need to stay awake late, I'll set an alarm and do ten push-ups every ten minutes. Works like a charm."

"I'll start with three and see how it goes," Tim said, still catching his breath.

Peter nodded, satisfied. Then, glancing at the stainless steel chronometer on his wrist, he said, "Ten minutes until dinner. How about we dive into the fourth action until Jacques lets us know it's time to eat?"

"I'm all ears!" Tim said eagerly. He pulled the old mahogany coffee table back into place, relieved to avoid more push-ups for now, and settled in for another round of note-taking.

HOW TO
GET STARTED

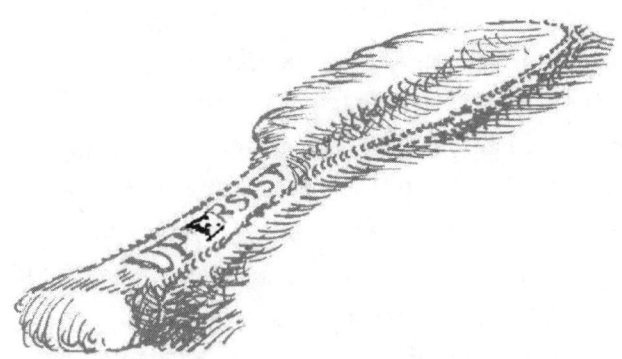

ACTION #3 | EXERCISE TO EXECUTE

What if I told you there was a pill that makes you smarter, helps you lose weight and build muscle, fights off depression, boosts your productivity, and prevents life-threatening conditions like heart disease and diabetes? How much would you pay—$10, $50, maybe $100?

Now, what if I told you this pill could change your destiny, making you successful and maybe even famous, if fame is your dream? And what if it gave you the confidence to do anything you set your mind to? What's the price now? $1,000? $10,000?

Let's sweeten the deal: What if the pill came with zero-percent financing? How much debt would you be willing to take on for this kind of power?

But wait—there's more! This pill could even help you attract the partner of your dreams. Take a moment to imagine the power of this pill. Close your eyes and picture it: Where would you go? What would you do? Who is the person of your dreams, and what would your life together look like? How would it feel to have that happiness? Would you change the world? What would you buy with your newfound wealth?

Now that you've dreamed about the incredible impact of this pill, here's the catch: for it to work, you need to set aside just thirty minutes a day.

That's it—thirty minutes. Does knowing about this small commitment change how much you value the pill? Probably not. In fact, you'd likely give up even more than thirty minutes for everything this pill offers.

Now think about your daily routines. How many things already take up thirty minutes or more? Getting ready for school or work, watching TV, scrolling through the internet, or reading the news.

Okay, here's the final catch: The pill doesn't work overnight. You need to take it daily—thirty days to *feel* a difference, sixty days to *see* a difference, and ninety days to *make* a difference. Still interested? What if I told you it's completely FREE? And there's no time limit on the offer.

The title of Action #3 probably gave away the kind of "pill" I'm talking about. The beauty of this metaphor, though, is that it's 100% true. Sure, exercise doesn't come in pill form, and yes, you'll need to put in some work during those thirty minutes. But exercise can be your secret weapon for achieving your dreams.

I'm living proof. Exercise helped me overcome asthma and gave me the confidence to try out for my high-school rowing team. Success in rowing led to being recruited to the Naval Academy, where I found the courage to try out for the SEALs. As a SEAL, I became a student of exercise and learned to harness it to unlock my potential.

Exercise has been my swim buddy throughout life. It propelled me from the SEALs to business school, and eventually to inventing the Perfect Pushup. It's given me the confidence to face my fears, the strength and stamina to pursue my dreams, and yes—I even credit exercise for helping me attract the woman of my dreams.

I know I've simplified my Milestone Goals and emphasized exercise as a key driver, but I'm not saying exercise was the only thing that helped me overcome asthma, win rowing championships, graduate SEAL training, invent successful products, or find the love of my life. What I *am* saying is that every success began with exercise. It's been my catalyst for dreaming up new ideas, my fuel to pursue them, and the endurance to keep going when others quit. Exercise keeps my brain focused, my attitude positive, and it powers my call to action.

When I get stuck, I take a break and pop a thirty-minute exercise pill. Exercise clears my mind and helps me get unstuck. In SEAL training, our instructors gave us a simple solution when doubt clouded our minds: "When in doubt—push 'em out!" We hated the tens of thousands of push-ups we had to do, but they became a reliable tool throughout our careers. Even now, push-ups help me wake up in the morning, stay alert during long work stretches, or celebrate a success. (It may sound strange, but nothing ramps up enthusiasm like the endorphins—those can-do chemicals—that come from cranking out twenty push-ups!)

There's a reason push-ups are a staple exercise throughout SEAL training: They engage every major muscle group. Think about it: You start with a deep squat (working your legs), extend your legs back (engaging your core and back), hold a plank position (activating core, back, arms, and shoulders), then lower yourself and push back up (targeting chest, arms, and abs). Do this repeatedly, and your heart starts pumping hard—just like during a sprint.

On my longest submarine stint—33 days—push-ups kept me sane. My teammates and I played push-up games with a deck of cards, assigning each suit to a different push-up variation and seeing how many times we could get through the deck before collapsing. The last man still pushing won.

The beauty of push-ups is that you can do them anytime, anywhere. If Jack Palance can drop down and crank out push-ups while accepting an Academy Award, then so can we! I've even done 10 push-ups in the middle of a meeting to honor someone's achievement—it gets laughs, gives me a charge, and brightens the moment.

There are very few valid excuses to skip push-ups. I've seen double-leg amputee veterans knock them out—if they can do it, so can the rest of us. Push-ups not only burn fat and build muscle but also boost brain power. When you challenge your muscles and force your heart to pump blood between your legs and arms (through squatting, pushing, and standing up), your body releases endorphins.

These hormones are like a natural drug for the body. They calm and focus the mind, triggering the release of dopamine—the "happy hormone"—which promotes a positive attitude and fights depression. Endorphins can also improve sleep, enhance sex drive, and boost circulation, which sharpens brain function, helps process information, and ultimately makes us smarter.

The power of exercise is so overwhelmingly clear and well-documented that I seriously considered dedicating this entire book to inspiring people to use it to their advantage. But life isn't as simple as doing push-ups. To achieve a Milestone Goal—a goal that will transform your life—you must commit to thousands of hours of action.

In *The Tipping Point*, Malcolm Gladwell argues that mastering a skill requires 10,000 hours of work. That's the equivalent of five years if you commit to a solid forty-hour work week for fifty weeks a year (everyone needs a vacation—two weeks off is a good thing). To sustain that level of focus and determination, you need stamina. And where do you think that stamina will come from? Coffee? Energy drinks?

Absolutely not! Those are quick fixes with long-term downsides. The sugar in energy drinks can lead to weight gain or even diabetes. They may give you a jolt of energy, but that's followed by a crash. The same applies to coffee—too much caffeine can cause headaches, jitters, heart palpitations, and fatigue. I enjoy coffee, but it's no substitute for the natural energy I generate through exercise.

To exercise is to execute. When you're stuck or unsure of what to do next, go exercise. It will not only recharge you but also give you a sense of accomplishment. That sense of achievement can help you shift to a positive mindset when you feel like giving up.

The most challenging obstacles you'll face are the ones in your mind. As Dr. Seuss wrote in *Oh, the Places You'll Go!*: "The toughest games you'll play are the games against yourself." These mental battles can only be won with a can-do attitude. It's normal to question yourself—humans are wired to avoid pain and seek pleasure. Work is inherently hard, but we persist for the rewards it brings.

The best way to win these mental games is to build a daily habit of working toward your goal. Strength, stamina, and energy are essential for staying on track, and the only way to develop them is through exercise.

Not sure where to start? No problem. Try this twenty-one-day plan to help you build an exercise habit and move closer to your goal. I recommend exercising first thing in the morning—it's too easy to push it off and make excuses later in the day. Don't make excuses—just do it!

Day 1: Find out how many push-ups you can do without stopping. Be honest—stop when you can no longer perform a push-up with perfect form. If you can't do a push-up from a plank position, no problem. Drop your knees to the floor and do as many as possible from that position. If even that feels too hard, start by using a bench, stairs, windowsill, or table—just make sure it's sturdy and won't move!

Day 2: Go for a 30-minute walk. If 30 minutes straight feels too daunting, break it into smaller chunks. If five minutes is all you can manage, do that six times throughout the day to reach your goal.

Day 3: Perform your maximum number of push-ups—one at a time. For example, if you can do 10, start by standing, squat down, do one push-up, stand back up, and repeat nine more times.

Day 4: Repeat Day 2.

Day 5: Repeat Day 3.

Day 6: Repeat Day 2.

Day 7: Have fun and go outside to play!

Day 8: Perform a maximum set of push-ups again. Afterward, stand up and try to do as many individual push-ups as possible, standing between each one. How many extra can you manage—three, five, seven, or more? Whatever the number, that's your new maximum.

Day 9: Go for a 30-minute walk. If you needed six five-minute increments on Day 2, you'll likely be able to complete the full 30 minutes all at once now.

Day 10: Complete your new maximum number of push-ups—one at a time. Stand between each one and knock them out with purpose.

Day 11: Repeat Day 9.

Day 12: Repeat Day 10.

Day 13: Repeat Day 9.

Day 14: Repeat Day 10.

Day 15: Go have fun!

Day 16: Perform one set maximum of push-ups. Afterward, stand up and see how many more individual push-ups you can do, standing between each one. Can you squeeze in two, three, four or more? Whatever the number, that's your new maximum.

Day 17: Go for a 30-minute walk. By now, you're likely covering more ground than you did on Day 2 or even Day 9.

Day 18: Complete your new maximum number of push-ups, one at a time, with a brief stand between each rep.

Day 19: Repeat Day 17.

Day 20: Repeat Day 18.

Day 21: Repeat Day 17.

Day 22: Get *Fired Up*! You're on your way to being unstoppable!

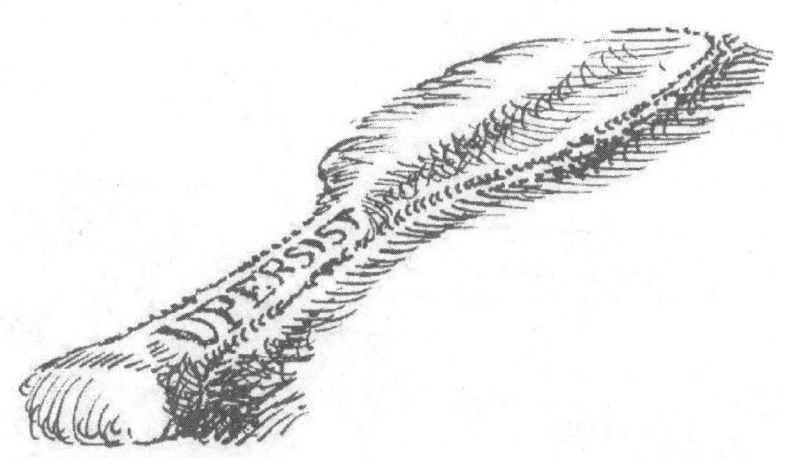

ACTION #4
Recognize Your Reason to Believe

The master and commander smiled, already anticipating the next question he would ask. Sitting motionless, Peter watched the young, out-of-breath captain collect himself after completing 10 push-ups. He remembered what it felt like to be a young captain—eager, full of energy, and hungry to learn. Though they hadn't yet covered all the actions of the code, Peter was certain Tim had what it took to follow it and become a master and commander in his own right.

Tim fidgeted nervously as the silence stretched on, sensing another soul-searching question was on the horizon. And he was right.

Peter leaned forward, resting his elbows on his thighs. "Tim, do you believe in yourself?"

The question hit Tim like a tidal wave, leaving him flustered and stranded. Tim glanced left and right as if looking for an escape, then rubbed his sweaty palms along his pant legs, stalling for time. "Like, do

I believe I'm 'Tim'?" he asked with a nervous half-smile, trying to make light of the question.

"No," Peter said, gaze unwavering. "I want to know whether you have *confidence* in yourself."

Tim squirmed under the weight of the question. "Sure, of course I believe in myself," he sputtered. Then, puffing out his cheeks like a blowfish and exhaling deeply, he confessed in a softer voice, "Not really." His head dropped as he avoided Peter's gaze.

Not wanting Tim to wallow a second longer, Peter clapped his hands sharply, snapping the young captain's attention back. "Of course not! You just ran your ship aground yesterday. And guess what? I know exactly how that feels. Heck, sandbars are nothing compared to rocks!"

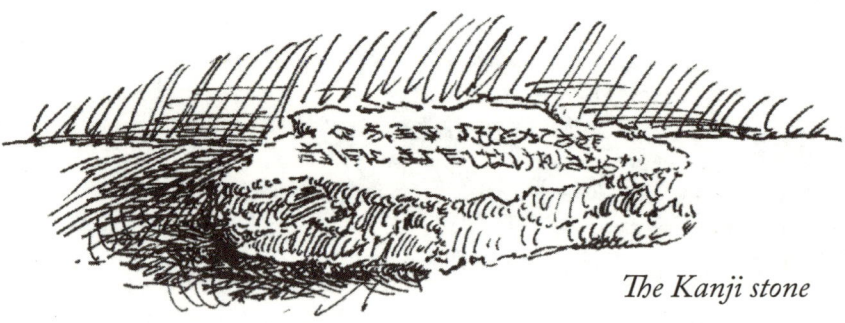

The Kanji stone

With that, Peter walked over to a tall display case behind his lounge chair. It stretched from floor to ceiling, bolted securely in place with stainless steel L-shaped brackets. Inside, four glass shelves—meant for medical supplies—held a collection of items. Peter opened the chest-high door and pulled out a large, flat rock.

"Take a look at this one," he said, placing the stone in front of Tim.

The oblong stone had a smooth blue-gray surface on one side, with something carved into it. Tim ran his fingers over the markings, curious. "What is this?"

"Those are Japanese kanji," Peter explained. "This stone was given to me by a Japanese master and commander."

RECOGNIZE YOUR REASON TO BELIEVE

"What does it say?" Tim asked, still admiring the smoothness of the stone.

"It says, *'Before you can achieve, you must first believe.'* I keep this stone on the third shelf of the display case so I see it every time I walk into the wardroom. I never want to forget those words."

Tim nodded, quietly repeating the phrase to himself as he reached for his notepad to write it down.

Peter continued, "The Japanese master compared the power of belief to a river—unstoppable in its journey. A river can flow over some obstacles, while it carves its way around others, gradually forging its own path. This stone is a perfect example; it came from the famous Fuji River, which flows from Mount Fuji to the sea. No matter how hard or solid the stone, the river's relentless flow eventually made it smooth."

Peter leaned closer, lowing his voice for emphasis. "*Relentless,* Tim. That's the key. A river's power isn't created all at once—it builds as it flows, becoming unstoppable over time. If you keep believing in yourself—no matter what—you'll find the strength to overcome any obstacle in your way, just like the river. Believe in yourself, Tim. And be relentless."

"So, all I have to do is believe, and I can achieve anything I want?" he asked skeptically.

Peter laughed. "If only it were that simple! First, you need to *recognize* a reason to believe—and that comes from the small successes in your life. These successes build on each other, giving you the confidence to tackle bigger, bolder tasks. It's like stacking bricks—one small success at a time until you build something substantial. Do you feel ready to leave Hardwork Harbor and cross the ocean with me tomorrow morning?"

Tim shifted uneasily in his chair.

"Of course not," Peter said with a grin. "You're not ready for that kind of voyage yet. But you *are* ready to cross the bay and make it to the south end of Hardwork Harbor."

Tim wasn't so sure—just thinking about it gave him butterflies. Peter noticed the hesitation.

"You must—and you will—cross that bay. You already know more about that course than you did the first time you tried. Now you know where that sandbar is."

Tim perked up. Peter was right. He'd spent so much time feeling embarrassed about being towed that he'd forgotten the valuable lesson he had learned—there was a sandbar between buoys 15 and 17.

Peter gave him a knowing look. "You want to know the real reason I exercise, Tim?"

Tim leaned in, curious.

"I exercise because it gives me more than strength and stamina. It gives me a reason to believe in myself."

Tim tilted his head, looking puzzled.

Peter nodded. "That's right. Exercise gives me the confidence to conquer whatever is within my control. When I was your age, just starting to learn the code, I was twenty-five pounds overweight. My master and commander gave me one simple task: *Take control of your body, and you'll take control of your life.*"

Peter paused, giving Tim time to scribble notes.

"I had nothing to lose—except weight—so I decided to start exercising. At first, all I got was a small rush of adrenaline and a bit of extra energy. But as my body started to change, my confidence grew.

"By the time I lost those twenty-five pounds, I wasn't even thinking about weight loss anymore. Instead, I was thinking about how to use this newfound power—this belief in myself—to tackle bigger and bolder challenges. That's when the idea of crossing an ocean stopped being a dream and started feeling possible."

The young captain sat silently, staring at his teacher, unsure of what to say. Peter noticed Tim's incredulous look and continued, "Whether you're trying to lose twenty-five pounds or sail twenty-five hundred miles across an ocean, it all starts with believing you can do it. You won't lose twenty-five pounds in a day, and your ship won't cover twenty-five hundred miles in one either. This stone," Peter said, running his hand over its surface, "wasn't smoothed in a day. But through relentless action, you will cross that ocean."

He paused, letting his hand mimic the flow of the river over the stone. "To sustain relentless action, you must believe in yourself and in the goal you're working toward. The stronger your belief, the harder you'll try—and when that happens, you'll discover there's nothing you can't do. The trick is learning to separate the beliefs that help you from the ones that hold you back."

Tim shifted suddenly, as if dodging a punch. "Wait, Captain! I followed you when you talked about finding a reason to believe in order to succeed, but what do you mean by beliefs that *hinder* me?"

Peter leaned forward, using his hands for emphasis. "Throughout our lives, we develop beliefs to help us survive and thrive. But some of those beliefs can get in the way of future goals. When that happens, they can slow your progress—or stop it altogether. Sometimes, long-held beliefs keep us from even trying a new course."

Tim's eyes narrowed as Peter's words sank in.

"What we believe dictates our actions, Tim. If you believe you can't cross the bay tomorrow, you won't take the steps to do it. But here's the good news: You've already crossed the bay once, so you know you *can*. And over time, the belief that got you across the bay will grow into a belief that you can cross any ocean."

Peter's tone softened, but his words were firm. "The key is to recognize and focus on the beliefs that support your chosen course. It's easier said than done."

He leaned back for a moment, his expression clouding as he reflected on a painful memory—his boat, stranded on the rocks. "There have been many times in my life when I believed I couldn't do something," he admitted.

Tim leaned in, his voice low and cautious, as if bracing for a trick. "What?"

"Every time I believed I couldn't do something, I was right," Peter said. "That 'can't' led me to take half-hearted action—or worse, none. Before I knew it, that belief became a self-fulfilling prophecy."

Peter leaned forward, his energy intensifying as his voice rose with excitement. "But the opposite is also true. Every time I believed I *could* do something I made progress toward my goal. Sometimes, it didn't feel like progress—I often just learned what *not* to do. But it was still progress because I kept believing I could do it! Get it?"

He paused just long enough for Tim to nod.

"Tim, remember what I told you earlier: *'Whether you believe you can or you can't, you're right.'*"

Tim's lips moved silently as he repeated the words to himself. Slowly, a smile began to spread from the corner of his mouth. "I . . . I think I'm tracking with you," he said. "My beliefs drive my actions—or my inactions—depending on what I believe I can or can't do. And what I can or can't do is entirely determined by what I believe, right?"

"Dead-on and Full Speed Ahead, Captain!" Peter exclaimed, jumping to his feet and clapping his hands in a single thunderous motion. "What you believe dictates what you can or can't achieve!"

Tim leaned back in his chair, feeling both relieved and enlightened. Peter could see the shift in him—this was the perfect moment to deliver the next part of his message.

Placing both hands gently on the smooth river stone, Peter lowered his head to meet Tim at eye level.

"The code is all about developing habits that help you succeed at the things you *can* control. You can't control the wind, water, or waves, but you *can* control how you respond to them. You can control the course you choose. Most importantly, you can control your actions—and your belief in yourself. Once you truly grasp this, you'll succeed at anything you set your mind to.

"And then, my friend," Peter continued with a grin, "the oceans and all their abundance will be your oysters—just waiting for you to harvest them. The oceans will test you, frustrate you, and challenge you, but they will also shape you into a more knowledgeable and capable captain.

"Trust me, Tim: If you follow the code and never stop believing in yourself and your course, you will be unstoppable in living your dreams."

A broad smile spread across Tim's face. No one had ever spoken to him with such positivity and encouragement. His heart rate quickened, and goose bumps rose along his forearms and at the nape of his neck. The commander's message was simple yet profound: Start with small successes, build a reason to believe, and never stop believing. With that, anything could become possible.

Behind the ruby-red curtain at the entrance to the galley, Jacques waited patiently. The old chef knew how rare these moments were—the master and commander only shared this speech on special occasions. Jacques admired his captain's passion for inspiring the next generation to follow their own paths. Though dinner had been ready for five extra minutes, the chef knew the commander wouldn't mind. He always enjoyed hearing the code repeated—it had guided Jacques in following his own course to becoming a chef.

As Peter leaned back, watching his student absorb the lesson, Jacques gently cleared his throat. He reached for a small brass ship's bell hanging beside the commander's war chest and gave it a soft chime. "Gentlemen, dinner is served," he announced. "Please lay to the mess for the evening meal."

The words lingered in the air as both captains paused, exchanging a look of mutual respect. Tim now had a deeper appreciation for his lessons and for the friendship he was building with Peter. The older captain admired his apprentice's courage and desire to chart his own course.

In truth, Peter may have gained more from the evening than Tim. Few things brought the aging master and commander greater joy than helping others pursue their own paths.

The master and commander moved first. "Okay, Tim, let's not keep Jacques's masterpieces waiting. Trust me, you don't want to upset the chef—or your palate. You're in for a real treat!" Peter motioned for Tim to bring the river rock to the table as he headed toward the feast. Along the way, he asked Jacques what was on the menu.

"Sir, tonight's meal begins with a local short-spined purple sea urchin, accompanied by slices of albacore tuna belly lightly brushed with Meyer lemon, ginger, and fresh soy sauce," Jacques announced proudly, stepping back from his creation. It looked more like an exotic flower than food.

Tim almost dropped the stone when he saw the precise arrangement of the meal. Though the round table could seat six, only two chairs were set—one at the four o'clock position, the other at eight o'clock, both facing the bow of the *Persistence*. Peter took the seat at eight o'clock.

A striking cloth divided the table from the three to nine o'clock position. Woven with interlocking diamond-shaped patterns, the fabric was a rich blend of red, blue, black, and white. Three candles, each cradled in small, opposing tusks, rested along the cloth's center. They flanked a large wooden bowl brimming with an assortment of fruits—some so exotic that Tim didn't recognize them.

Tim was still marveling at the table's intricate design when Peter's playful voice cut through his thoughts. "Time, tide, and Jacques's meals wait for no one. Let's eat, skipper!"

"Aye, aye, captain!" Tim responded with enthusiasm.

As he prepared to dive into the meal, Tim tried to ready his taste buds, but his brain couldn't process the exotic flavors he was about to experience. He had never encountered such a divine spectacle on a plate. While deciding where to begin, Peter offered a suggestion.

"May I recommend alternating between the sea urchin and the tuna? The urchin is salty, while the tuna melts like sweet butter," Peter said, lifting an iridescent spoon carved from abalone shell. With care, he scooped a bit of urchin meat from the belly of the spiny delicacy.

Tim followed Peter's lead, and the flavors amazed him, blending in perfect harmony on his tongue.

A few bites into the appetizer, Peter broke the silence with a grin. "Bravo, Jacques. You've outdone yourself again. Outstanding!"

From the galley, Jacques peeked around the corner, smiling warmly. "Why, thank you, captain. The next course will be served in eight minutes, sir."

Tim couldn't help but admire Jacques's precision—from his exact timing to the artistry of the first course. The chef's perfectionism was impossible to miss.

As they savored the food, Peter's gaze fell on the "believe to achieve" stone, which Tim had placed between them on the table. Without missing a beat, Peter slipped back into teaching mode.

"So, let's recap before Jacques interrupts us with another culinary masterpiece," Peter said with a playful wink, just loud enough for the chef to hear.

"I'll do my best, cap'n," Jacques replied from the galley. "Seven minutes and counting, sir."

Peter grinned at Tim. "I call Action #4 'Recognize Your Reason to Believe.' Remember the lesson of the stone—and how a relentless river carves its way over time. To achieve, you must believe. Believing starts with small successes, which grow into bigger ones. And the more you succeed, the more you'll believe in yourself. The stronger your belief, the more unstoppable you'll become."

Peter's voice dropped an octave as he said the word *unstoppable,* his tone carrying the weight of experience and truth. The intensity startled Tim.

"And when you're unstoppable, nothing can stop you from following your course and achieving your dreams," Peter continued. "You'll never give up. When you learn how to maintain your course and speed, no matter what life throws at you, you'll become your own master and commander."

Tim dropped his spoon and furiously scribbled in his notepad. "I'm reading you loud and clear! I get Action #4! Believing leads to achieving because it keeps you going when others give up. It's like confidence fuel to power through rough waters when the course gets tough."

Peter beamed with pride. "Exactly, Tim!"

Tim nodded, the pieces clicking into place. "Actions one, two, and three build habits that teach you to believe in yourself, giving you the confidence to keep going and not quit." His voice trailed off as a realization took hold.

And then it hit him.

"Persistence!" Tim shouted triumphantly.

Peter leaned back in his chair, grinning ear to ear, savoring Tim's moment of reckoning.

"You named your ship after the meaning of the code," Tim said in dawning realization. "You must see that word a thousand times a day. You did it so you'll never forget what it's all about, didn't you? Just like this stone—you put it here to remind yourself constantly of the code!"

Peter smiled and nodded. "When I first learned the code, I was so inspired that I promised myself I'd never forget what it stands for. What better way to keep it front and center than naming my ship *Persistence*?"

"That's a serious commitment to the code."

"It is," Peter agreed. "But as you'll soon see, success comes from building habits that push you toward your dream. I wanted a habit that wouldn't just remind me occasionally but one that would stay with me every day and every hour. And I wanted it out in the world for everyone to see.

"I wasn't the best student, or the best athlete—and I wasn't even the best ship driver. But I made it my mission to be the best at one thing: never giving up. I committed to dreaming big and holding myself accountable for making those dreams a reality. Naming the ship *Persistence* was a small but powerful way to reinforce the habit of remembering what it takes to succeed—every single day."

Tim listened in awe, impressed not only by Peter's passion for persistence but also by his humility. Here was a man who had once been ordinary but worked extraordinarily hard to shape the life he wanted. The more Tim heard, the more he wanted a life like Peter's.

His teacher gave his student a thoughtful look. "I hadn't planned to show you this yet, Tim, but since you've put two and two together about the code, I think now's the time."

He motioned for Tim to follow him and called out to Jacques. "How's the timing, Jacques?"

"Three and a half minutes, sir," came the prompt reply.

Peter nodded and led Tim to a hidden mahogany-paneled door to the left of a vintage oil painting. The painting depicted a ship braving stormy seas, a ray of light piercing through the dark clouds, as if guiding the vessel through the tempest.

Peter pressed the panel, and with a soft hiss, the door opened, releasing a breeze of fresh sea air. They stepped onto the bridge of the *Persistence*, directly behind the helm. Peter flipped on the red navigation lights and pointed to a plaque beneath the compass.

"Go ahead, Tim. Read it out loud."

Together, they recited the words:

"Nothing in the world can take the place of persistence. Talent will not; nothing is more common than unsuccessful men with talent. Genius will not; unrewarded genius is almost a proverb. Education will not; the world is full of educated derelicts. Persistence and determination alone are omnipotent. The slogan 'Press On' has solved and always will solve the problems of the human race."

Tim stood tall, turning to Peter with renewed respect. He extended his hand and said earnestly, "Thank you, Peter. Thank you for showing me the way."

"The pleasure and the honor are all mine," Peter replied, gripping Tim's hand firmly. "Now, let's not keep Jacques waiting. We might still catch him before he slips back into the galley."

They returned to the table, Tim trying to burn the words from the plaque into his memory but coming up short. Sensing this, Peter quietly repeated the inscription, finishing just as Jacques reappeared.

"Gentlemen," Jacques announced with pride, "tonight's main course is pan-seared ahi tuna, seasoned with wasabi, olive oil, and kosher salt, then glazed with soy sauce. It's served with a chilled seaweed salad and sushi rice. Should you need anything, just call out. Enjoy, gentlemen."

With a quick 180-degree turn, Jacques whisked the appetizer plates away and disappeared into the galley.

Neither captain spoke as they closed their eyes, allowing their senses to fully absorb the dish's intoxicating aroma. Tim was still processing the symphony of scents when Peter said with a grin, "Well, no time like the present—let's eat!"

HOW TO
GET STARTED

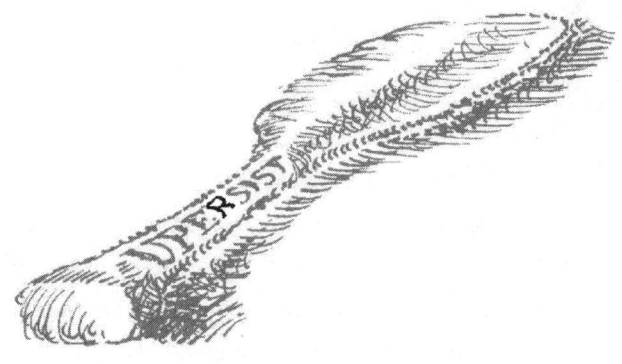

ACTION #4 | RECOGNIZE YOUR REASON TO BELIEVE

The first team sport I ever played was basketball at the local YMCA. Our teams were named after NBA franchises, and our uniforms mimicked the pros—meaning in the 1970s we wore tank tops, tube socks, and shorts—*really* short shorts. The tops fit tight, the socks came up to our knees, and the shorts showed most of our thighs. While most of the other eight-year-olds didn't mind the uniforms, I hated them. My thighs were huge, and compared to the skinny legs of the other players I stuck out.

The nicknames started as soon as I put those YMCA shorts on: "Tree Trunks," "Log Legs," and the one that stuck—"Thunder Thighs." Being a poor basketball player didn't help, nor did my inability to jump more than a couple of inches off the ground. The nickname followed me from the basketball court to the elementary school playground, where tag was the sport of choice. There, I learned I wasn't much better at running fast either.

Over time, I accepted the nickname—there wasn't much I could do about the size of my thighs. My mom would tell me, "They're just jealous of your big, powerful legs." But I wasn't always convinced.

Through eighth grade, I did my best to ignore the name Thunder Thighs. But it wasn't easy, especially since I struggled at the traditional sports—football, soccer, basketball, and baseball. That made me an easy target. Things began to change, though, when I started high school, and I found a sport that didn't require kicking, pitching, dribbling, or catching—a sport done on water: rowing.

I'll never forget my first day of club rowing. Our coach, Professor Johnson, picked me out of the lineup of freshmen and said, "Mills, you've got the legs of an oarsman—big and strong."

That statement completely changed how I viewed my thunder thighs. Suddenly, they weren't something to be embarrassed about—they were an asset. They became my reason to believe in myself, and that belief gave me the confidence to try out for the varsity rowing team the next year. I didn't have the same rowing experience, upper-body strength, or lung capacity as the other rowers, but I knew one thing: *I had the legs for it.*

At the start of my sophomore year, I teamed up with a senior who agreed to train with me. I dropped all my other sports and focused entirely on rowing for the next seven months. Every waking moment was spent thinking about how to earn a seat on one of the two Kent School Boat Club (KSBC) boats.

I had no idea at the time just how steep the competition would be. KSBC had a storied history, with Coach W. Hart Perry Jr. leading the way. His crews had won more championships than any other high school rowing program, and students came from all over the world to row for him. Earning one of the 16 seats—eight per boat—was no small feat.

Six of the varsity rowers were returning from the previous year, and all eight seats on the second boat were filled by returning rowers. That left only two open spots, and one was almost certainly going to a sophomore whose brother was already on the first boat—and who had prior rowing experience.

Realistically, that left just one open seat. If I'd made a list of reasons why I shouldn't make the team, it would've been long:

- I had the least rowing experience.
- I couldn't do that many pull-ups (a key tryout exercise).
- I had asthma.

On the other hand, my "why I can make KSBC" list had just one bullet point:

- *I believe I can make it because I was born with rower's legs.*

There comes a moment in every challenging situation when you have to dig deep and find the resolve to keep going. That moment came for me on the final day of rowing tryouts in Tampa, Florida. I was rowing in the bow of an eight-man boat, racing against another KSBC tryout crew. If we won, the seat would be mine. If we lost, I'd go home.

The two-a-day practices in Florida had been brutal, and my hands weren't used to the endless hours of gripping a wooden handle. Blisters had formed on every finger, then popped, leaving raw, infected sores. I had to tape my hands into claw-like shapes, sliding the oar handle through the small circle I could still manage to hold.

Midway through the race, a wave crashed over the bow and onto my back, drenching my hands with salt water. The burning was instant and fierce as the seawater soaked through the tape, stinging the open sores. Tears welled up and streamed down my face as I fought to push through the pain.

Every pull on the oar felt like fire in my hands, but I knew this was my defining moment—the moment I had to find my reason to believe. As much as the salt water burned, the thought of not earning that seat hurt even more.

Every day of training had brought me to this point—this last race, this final chance to earn my spot. I believed I could do it, and nothing else mattered—not the pain in my hands, the unfair wave, or the burn in my lungs.

We won the race, and I earned my seat that day. My life changed forever. I had learned what it meant to believe in myself. As simple as it sounds, my big thighs—once a source of embarrassment—had become my reason to believe in making the rowing team.

It doesn't matter where your reason to believe comes from; what matters is that you recognize it. That belief is your secret weapon for success, no matter how big the odds are against you.

I still remember classmates laughing when I said I would try out as a sophomore for KSBC. Every odd was against me—except one. The only one that mattered: my reason to believe.

Our great Coach Perry always told us before every race, "A crew must first believe before they can achieve."

At the Naval Academy, Coach Clothier—another legendary rowing coach—had a simple philosophy. His crews would row 2,000 miles a year—one mile for every meter of a standard 2,000-meter race course. His logic? He wanted us to be in better shape than any other crew we faced. He knew no other team would log as many miles. The goal was to give us confidence—our reason to believe we could win was that we had trained harder than anyone else.

In SEAL training, my reasons to believe came from many different sources. With so many challenges, I had to find a reason to believe in everything I did. For the diving tests, my reason to believe came from earning my scuba certification with my dad at the age of twelve. For the shooting tests, I drew confidence from winning rifle competitions at summer camp. Rope climbs and pull-up competitions? My strength came from rowing.

When it came to surf torture—enduring the freezing water—my reason to believe came from winter rowing sessions on the Severn River at the Naval Academy. Running long distances? Rowing had prepared me for that too. In fact, most of my reasons for believing I could survive SEAL training were rooted in rowing.

I knew I wouldn't be the fastest runner or swimmer, nor the strongest at push-ups or pull-ups, but I also knew that I could endure more than most. During runs or swims, when I found myself at the back of the pack, I'd give myself the same pep talk every time: *"Just keep going—one step or one stroke at a time. I can do one more..."*

That simple mantra carried me through every challenge. One more stride would turn into another, and then another, until I reached the finish line.

I became a master of breaking things down into manageable steps. No matter what the instructors threw at me, I found comfort in my reason to believe that I could handle it. I would approach every challenge the same way I approached rowing—one stroke at a time. Just keep going. Just keep pulling.

SEALs understand how critical it is to believe in yourself and your teammates. That's why both officers and enlisted men go through the same training. Though it serves as just the starting point, this shared experience gives enlisted SEALs a reason to believe in their officers. But belief alone isn't enough—officers must earn respect through consistent, sound decision-making and leadership. It's also why Hellweek is so grueling. After enduring a week designed to simulate the intensity of combat, SEALs leave with a reason to believe they can handle the real thing.

Finding your reason to believe is essential for achieving any goal. To accomplish something, you must first believe that you *can* achieve it.

The key to recognizing your reason to believe is to focus on something you know to be true. In ninth grade, I knew without a doubt that I had big legs. Then a teacher told me that big legs were great for rowing—and that single connection gave me a reason to believe I could make the rowing team as a sophomore.

From there, I built on that belief, becoming a better rower, then a Navy SEAL. Each success along the way reinforced my reason to believe that I could take on even greater challenges—like starting a business.

When faced with bankruptcy, I didn't dwell on the possibility of failure. Instead, I immediately tapped into my reason to believe that I wouldn't give up just because the business ran out of money. Memories of rowing challenges and SEAL training flooded my mind, reminding me that I'd endured worse.

That belief gave me the confidence to push forward, and it encouraged my team to do the same. Together, we found a way to keep the business afloat.

The power of recognizing your reason to believe is that it not only carries you through your darkest, most difficult moments—it also inspires others to stick with you. Belief is contagious. When you share your reason to believe with others, you multiply your chances of success.

We all want to believe in something, and there's no better person to believe in than yourself.

Believe to achieve!

EXERCISE
FINDING YOUR REASON TO BELIEVE

Ask at least three different people this question:

"If I were going to save your life using my best skill—whatever you think I'm best at—how would I do it?"

This exercise will help you discover what others see as your unique strength—your gift, so to speak. Their feedback can serve as your initial reason to believe as you embark on a new goal.

As you commit to the journey and take consistent action, you'll uncover even more reasons to believe in yourself. One success will build upon another, and before you know it, your belief will become unshakable.

ACTION #5
Survey Your Habits

A few moments passed as Tim and Peter enjoyed the exquisite meal Jacques had prepared. Tim had never experienced anything so delicious—each bite seemed better than the last. He had to remind himself to slow down and savor the flavors.

As a natural pause settled between bites, Peter asked, "So, are you ready for the next action, skipper?"

"Standing by and ready to receive, sir," Tim replied, grinning.

"Alright, by now, you understand the importance of believing, right?"

Tim nodded vigorously, still savoring the buttery richness of the tuna.

"Good," Peter said, setting his utensils down. "This next action builds on the others. It's all about identifying obstacles—though not the kind you might expect. I'm not talking about rocks this time, but habits. These can be just as stubborn and dangerous. I'm referring to the habits you've created, either consciously or unconsciously, that are sabotaging your progress."

Peter paused to take another bite, giving Tim a chance to jot down notes. Tim drew a thick horizontal line across the page and wrote "Action #5" at the top.

"Tim, I mentioned this earlier—your daily actions form your habits. And whether good or bad, they're just sequences of actions your brain has decided to execute automatically. They shape what you do every day. The key is to recognize which ones are holding you back and modify them so they no longer stand in your way."

Tim nodded thoughtfully, pen hovering over the page. "Can you give me an example of a good habit and a bad habit?"

"Remember when I told you about my first attempt to leave the harbor and how I almost sank from taking on so much water?"

Tim shuddered, recalling the story. "The time you deliberately ran your ship aground?"

"That's the one. Do you know why I took on so much water?"

Tim thought for a moment. "You had a hatch open near the waterline?" he guessed.

"Not just one hatch—four. And remember, I also lost a bunch of gear, including my tow line."

Tim grimaced at the thought and gave a slow nod.

Peter leaned forward. "I lost that gear and took on water because I'd developed some bad habits without even realizing it. I had a habit of not latching a hatch immediately after opening it, and I wouldn't tie down gear right after using it. I kept telling myself, 'I'll latch that hatch later,' or, 'I'll secure that gear in a bit.' But later came and went—and I'd forget. Those habits caught up with me the day I tried to leave the harbor."

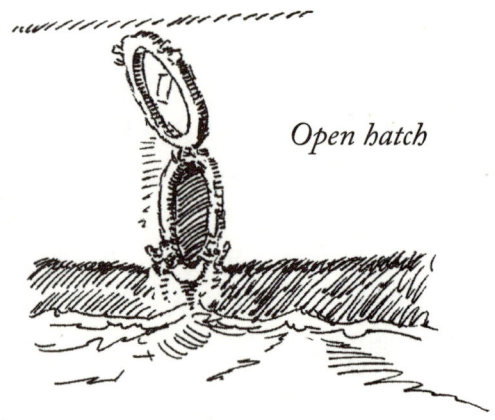

Open hatch

Peter chuckled. "The funny thing is, I didn't even realize those were bad habits until the master and commander teaching me the code pointed them out. She said, 'You're not going to get very far if you can't latch a hatch every time you go through it.' And she wasn't kidding—she made me practice it a hundred times."

"Come on! She really made you go through a hatch, latch it, and repeat that a hundred times?"

Peter grinned. "I swear on King Neptune's trident. She grabbed a big mug of coffee, perched herself on the bridge wing, and counted every single latched hatch."

He leaned back, chuckling at the memory. "At the time, I didn't appreciate what she was doing for me. She was helping me reprogram a bad habit—drilling it into me through sheer repetition."

Peter's grin widened as he recalled her parting words. "When I finished the task, she looked at me, smiled, and said, *'The mother of perfection is perfect repetition.'*"

Peter sat up straight, eyes gleaming. "And since that day, I've never left a hatch unlatched."

Peter paused for another bite as Tim jotted down the quote. He circled it, signaling Peter to continue.

"Latching a hatch is an essential tactical habit at sea. I say 'tactical' because it takes hundreds of these habits to keep a ship afloat—tying down gear, maintaining engines, checking for leaks, and so on. But you need *strategic* habits to stay on course. It's up to you to set your course and stick with it. Staying focused and motivated is a habit too—just like latching a hatch. The trick is identifying the strategic habits that will keep you on track. That's where exercise comes in. It's not just a good habit; it's a strategic one."

Tim, fully onboard with the logic, added, "Like making believing a habit!"

Peter smiled. "Exactly. That's a very strategic habit."

Tim's confidence had grown throughout the evening. He no longer feared the captain's questions; he was catching on.

"But remember, it's easier said than done. I use exercise to fuel belief in myself—it's the keel that keeps me positive. It helps me search for the light in any storm I encounter." Peter gestured toward the painting Tim had noticed earlier. "I keep that painting where I can see it every meal to remind me: no storm lasts forever. Every storm has its light—you just have to find it. And the only way to find it is to keep looking, just like the captain in the painting."

Peter pointed to a figure Tim hadn't noticed before—a man in dark rain slickers standing proudly behind the helm. As Tim leaned closer, he asked, "Is he smiling?"

Peter nodded. "Good catch."

"I don't get it. The artist must've never been at sea—there's nothing to smile about in waves like that. Those must be twenty-footers!" Tim exclaimed.

"The artist *was* the skipper," Peter said calmly.

"What? Who smiles in a storm like that?" Tim scoffed.

"What if he welcomed the storm?"

"I'd say you and the captain both lost your compasses. Why would anyone want to ride through a storm like that?"

"A captain who wanted to test his ship's improvements, that's who," Peter answered. "As the captain who taught me the code used to say, 'Always welcome adversity—there's no better teacher.' She always found light in storms and credited her success to the habit of 'never stop learning.'"

Peter pointed to a small brass plaque centered on the painting's frame. Tim leaned in and read: **"Prepare for the worst. Expect the best. Take what comes."**

"Tim, this captain didn't have a death wish, and this wasn't his first storm," Peter said. "He'd weathered many storms before this one—and wasn't prepared for most of them. He once told me about the white-knuckled fear he felt during his first storm outside the safety of a harbor. But afterward, he realized how good it felt to ride it out. That sense of accomplishment changed him. He came to see storms as opportunities to learn and excel. Now, ask yourself: What would you do, and more importantly, how would you feel if you treated every adversity as an opportunity to excel?"

Peter drifted back to the table, where the rest of his tuna steak waited. Tim kept studying the painting, his gaze shifting between the captain's smile and the inscription. He couldn't detect even a hint of fear in the captain's face. It was hard to believe anyone would welcome a storm like the one in the painting. Slowly, Tim turned and asked, "The storms also gave this captain something else, didn't they?"

Peter, mid-bite, raised his eyebrows and tilted his head, encouraging Tim to continue.

"The storms gave him a reason to believe," Tim said.

Peter swallowed quickly, eager to reward the insight. "Exactly! The storm is a symbol of adversity. We all face it in life. The key isn't to fear it but to learn from it. And to do that, you need habits that keep your mind open to new lessons and maintain your positivity so the storm never gets the better of you."

Tim smiled as he returned to his seat to finish the last of his meal. The code's logic was clicking into place. Each lesson built on the one before, all revolving around controlling what you could. And when control wasn't possible—like in a storm—you'd do your best, learn from it, and come out better prepared for the next one. No wonder that skipper was smiling. Tim thought to himself, *I'd smile too if I knew I could ride out a storm like that.*

The two men sat quietly, savoring the last bites of their meal. While eating, Tim jotted down the inscription from the painting, slightly tweaking it: **"Prepare for the worst, expect the best, take what comes with a smile."**

Tim finished first and leaned in. "So, what other habits did you focus on to face adversity and find success?"

"Well, I already mentioned exercise," Peter began. "I believe it's a life-changing habit with countless benefits. It gives you the strength and stamina to work harder for longer. It keeps you healthy, so you visit sick bay far less than those who don't. And it's proven to fight depression. But the toughest storms you'll face, Tim, aren't the ones at sea—they're the ones between your ears." Peter paused, waiting to see if Tim would catch the metaphor.

Tim shifted his gaze to the fruit bowl in the middle of the table, nodding slowly as Peter's words sank in. Just twenty-four hours ago, he'd felt like giving up after hitting that sandbar. The put-downs from so-called friends like Ted had dragged him down, making him question himself so deeply that he'd considered never leaving his ship again. But Peter had come along and flipped his perspective, helping Tim see the positive side of hitting that sandbar. Tim realized he needed to build a habit of staying positive, so no matter what he faced he wouldn't feel defeated.

"I get how important it is to keep a positive mindset," said Tim.

"When I say 'positive,' I don't mean being a cheerleader, though that has its place," Peter replied. "I mean always searching for the positive—what you can learn—no matter what comes your way. Got it?"

"Loud and clear. So, besides exercise, what other habits helped you succeed?" Tim leaned in, eager for more.

Peter smiled at Tim's enthusiasm. "The code, of course! The more you practice it, the more you'll see how it builds habits that lead to success, whatever course you choose. The code is just a framework. You have to set the course and summon the courage. It provides a plan for chasing your dreams, but the effort, imagination, and work? That's on you. The code's only as good as your willingness to live by it."

"I'm all in. I just want to know if there are other habits I should keep in mind."

"There are," Peter nodded. "You also need to be vigilant about habits that steer you off course. Unhealthy habits, like drinking or using drugs, can sink you before you even leave the harbor. Dishonorable habits—lying, cheating, stealing—will destroy your integrity and with it your chances of success. We all make mistakes. When you do, be like the captain in that painting," Peter said, gesturing toward the smiling skipper. "Take responsibility. Face your mistakes head-on. Steer into the wave and deal with it. Keep your speed steady and don't look back. Always focus on the next wave."

Tim absorbed the advice, then asked, "So, what's Action #5? 'Find bad habits'?"

"Close," Peter said. "I call it 'Survey Your Habits.' Remember, actions create habits. If you make a habit of surveying your actions, you'll catch bad habits before they knock you off course. Make sense?"

"Yes. A whole boatload," Tim replied.

"Good. The last three actions build on Action #5. It's critical to understand: Actions are the building blocks of habits. You control your actions, which means you own your habits. Are you with me?"

"I am, skipper. Ready for your next transmission," Tim said eagerly.

Peter grinned. "Very well, Captain Tim. Let's kick off the next action with a little show-and-tell, shall we?"

HOW TO
GET STARTED

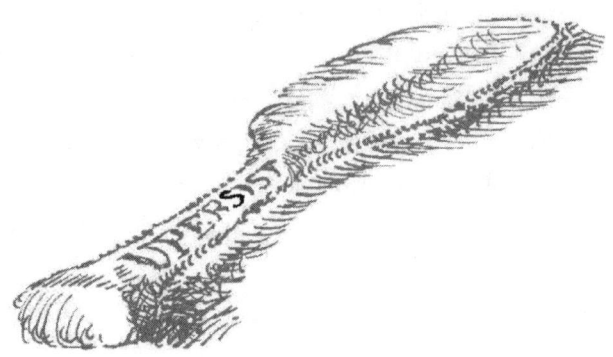

ACTION #5 | SURVEY YOUR HABITS

SEAL training is divided into three phases—appropriately named first, second, and third. The big challenge in the first phase is Hellweek, which accounts for most voluntary dropouts. In the second phase, the Pool Competency Test (or "Pool Comp") is the main obstacle, responsible for the most involuntary dismissals. This test simulates a series of underwater emergencies, created and conducted by a team of enthusiastic SEAL instructors. Each scenario builds on the previous one, with the final exercise stripping you of access to your scuba tanks. By this point, you've been harassed by up to five instructors for over 20 minutes at the bottom of a nine-foot pool. Your adrenaline surges, your heart races, and between gulps of air and water, you lose your air supply entirely. Staying calm is essential—if you panic, you won't be able to hold your breath long enough to follow the procedures, ditch your gear, and pass the test.

I actually looked forward to Pool Comp—I've loved scuba diving since I was 12. I was so eager to get certified that I convinced my dad to be my swim buddy so I could meet the dive shop's requirement for having an adult present. At the time, 12 was the youngest age they would certify a diver. Once I earned my certification, I took every opportunity to dive. By the time I reached the second phase of SEAL training, I felt confident I could pass Pool Comp—I had a decade of diving experience under my belt. What I didn't realize was that I'd also developed 10 years of bad diving habits.

Part of what makes SEAL training so difficult is the unfamiliarity. Nothing feels routine. The uniforms are from the 1940s. The only swim stroke allowed is the underwater recovery stroke—a modified side stroke that's faster but unlike anything I'd used before. The obstacle course is unlike any other, the boats are relics, and the exercises? Well, let's just say I'd never worked out with a telephone pole until SEAL training.

Even the dive gear was different. Instead of a modern setup with a single hose and a second stage in front of your mouth, SEAL tanks come with two 80-cubic-inch cylinders. The first and second stages are inconveniently mounted behind your head, and two soft black tubes protrude from either side—one for inhaling on the right and one for exhaling on the left. Using this setup was a completely new experience for me.

Though the gear was different, my confidence remained high. It was just scuba gear—no big deal. I figured I'd adapt and rely on my usual diving habits. That was the wrong mindset, and, worse, the habits I had developed over a decade of diving were not the ones the SEAL instructors wanted to instill in us as potential combat divers. I learned that the hard way.

Pool Comp takes place on a Friday, with three chances to pass—two on Friday and one final shot on Monday. My first attempt on Friday morning barely lasted ninety seconds. Two instructors rolled me, loosened my tank straps, and waited to see how I'd respond. My first instinct was wrong—I dropped my weight belt. That earned me a tap on the head, signaling me to surface. When I emerged, they told me to sit on the edge of the pool, facing away so I couldn't watch what happened next.

That afternoon, I did slightly better, lasting about three and a half minutes. But once again, I dropped my weight belt and was told to leave the pool. Not good—I had just one chance left on Monday. If I failed, I'd be packing my sea bag for a five-year tour on an "oiler" (Navy slang for a fuel ship).

That weekend, a veteran SEAL instructor hosted a remedial session for those of us who had failed Pool Comp twice. We called him Instructor Aloha (not his real name). He was from Hawaii, a big-wave surfer with a double dose of Aloha spirit. His method for preparing us was unorthodox—it had nothing to do with water, even though the entire test was in the pool. Instead, he focused on rewiring our bad habits through land drills in the SEAL command parking lot.

"The problem isn't the water," Aloha explained. "It's what you do when you're short of air that's holding you back."

His drills were designed to get us comfortable with the discomfort of running out of air. The first exercise was a simple game of hide and seek using common dive gear—a fin, mask, and snorkel, which he labeled objects one, two, and three. He placed them in plain sight but spaced just far enough apart that we had to run to gather them all on one breath.

At first, it was easy. We just had to pace ourselves. But Aloha gradually raised the stakes, adding a pause before giving the signal to start, forcing us to use up more air. In the final round, he changed the sequence in which we had to collect the objects, keeping us on our toes.

One at a time, we stood at the imaginary starting line, holding our breath, waiting to hear the required pickup sequence—something like "three, one, two." With just three objects, the task was straightforward. But when the number increased to five, things got a lot more complicated. We had to remember where each object was, the number assigned to it, and the order in which to pick them up—all while starving our brains of oxygen. More than one of us passed out during the game (myself included).

At first, the game didn't make much sense. But by the end, its brilliance became clear: it was training us to think under pressure—or more specifically, to think with limited air.

Once we had all completed the game to Aloha's satisfaction (which took most of Saturday), he assigned numbers to the steps needed to manage our dive gear. Then, holding our breath, we rehearsed those steps until they became automatic. We didn't realize it at the time, but he was rewiring our bad habits, replacing them with the good ones we needed to pass Pool Comp. By breaking our habits into individual actions, rearranging them under pressure, and reinforcing them through repetition, he had effectively reprogrammed us.

The training paid off. I passed Pool Comp on Monday morning, along with several others from my class. Our failure rate was unusually low, and I credit that to Aloha's focus on rewiring habits, one action at a time.

Pool Comp wasn't the only place where SEAL instructors weeded out bad habits. Every one of us entered BUD/S with bad habits—some we knew about, others we didn't. Identifying and correcting obvious habits, like adjusting dive straps or practicing sight alignment and trigger control when shooting, was relatively straightforward. But other habits, like attitude and attention to detail, were harder to spot and fix.

As a SEAL officer, attitude and attention to detail are more critical than perfect marksmanship. Shooting the black out of a bull's-eye from 200 yards is great, but without the right mindset and focus, it won't get you far. The real challenge is recognizing which habits are holding you back—and that requires understanding how habits work.

Whether you aim to lead SEALs in combat, sing on a world stage, or sail the seven seas, the sooner you understand habits, the sooner you'll be on the path to success. A habit is nothing more than a sequence of actions. Almost every action you take belongs to a larger collection of behaviors. When those actions repeat over time, they become automatic—and that's a habit.

The good news is that habits are within your control. The key is identifying the habit you want to change, breaking down its actions, and replacing them with better ones. And sometimes, critical habits can form much faster than you'd expect. Take opening a parachute, for example—it didn't take me 21 days to build that habit! *The process of forming good habits is exactly the same as forming bad ones.*

There's a simple three-step process for building habits to help you achieve your goal. It's called ACT:

Aware: Be aware of the habit that's holding you back. If you're unsure what it is, ask a friend, teacher, or expert. Set your ego aside and take an honest look at actions you take for granted—success is in the details.

Concentrate:—Focus on the action or actions that need to change. If you're consistently late for work or school, you've developed a habit. Identify what's causing the delay and concentrate on a new action, like getting up ten minutes earlier.

Take control:—Once you've identified the action that needs changing, take control! Remember, every action you take is yours—you own it, and it's within your control to change. Don't get discouraged if it takes time; old habits can be tough to break, but it's absolutely possible. Your habits are *up to you*!

As you start applying the ACT framework, a funny thing happens: you'll build a habit of *surveying your habits*. And what better habit is there than one that drives continuous improvement?

If you want to dive deeper into the science of habits and how to reprogram them, I highly recommend reading *The Power of Habit* by Charles Duhigg and *Atomic Habits* by James Clear. Both are excellent resources that show how habits work—and how they're entirely within your control to shape.

EXERCISE
SURVEY YOUR HABITS

Learn to measure your progress when building a new habit. The better you are at tracking your progress, the easier it becomes to embrace change.

For example, if you want to improve your public speaking but have been told you use too many "ums" and "ahs," ask someone in the audience to count them for you. If you want to work on punctuality, give yourself a point every time you arrive early to an appointment and subtract a point whenever you're late. Track your score each day.

Have fun figuring out how to measure your new habit! The more actively you engage with tracking and learning, the faster you'll embrace the habit—and the sooner you'll find success.

ACTION #6
Improvise

Peter motioned for Tim to follow him as he called out to Jacques, complimenting him on a superb meal. Jacques immediately began clearing the table in preparation for dessert. Tim couldn't decide what he was more excited about—Peter's show-and-tell or Jacques's dessert. Peter informed Jacques that he and Tim would return in about ten minutes. Jacques gave a nod, gathering the plates and the wooden fruit bowl that had served as the centerpiece, then retreated to the galley.

As Tim stood still, admiring Jacques's efficiency, Peter gave him a nudge on the shoulder. "About face, sailor. I've got a couple of things to show you."

They left the warmth of the wardroom and descended into the belly of the *Persistence*. Entering the engine room, Peter pressed a circular green button by the starboard-side hatch. Within seconds, a small, muscular woman with cropped hair appeared from behind a bank of batteries. She wore a vest with tools stashed in its many pockets. For an engineer, she was surprisingly clean—Tim didn't spot a single grease mark on her clothing.

"Captain Tim, I have the pleasure of introducing you to Grace. She's the reason the *Persistence* runs like a dream."

"Jam-Bo! Captain Tim!" Grace greeted him in a bright, sing-song voice, radiating youthful energy. "Welcome to the pride of the *Persistence*!"

"You said it," Peter agreed. "Grace, we've only got a few minutes, but could you tell Tim about the battery system you invented for the *Persistence*?"

"With pleasure, cap'n!" Grace beamed.

Tim tilted his head toward Peter, surprised. He had assumed the invention was Peter's. Turning back to Grace, Tim couldn't help but marvel at how spotless the engine room was—it was unlike any he'd ever seen.

Grace pointed to two large banks of batteries. "One afternoon, I found the cap'n pacing the boat after we'd off-loaded some cargo. He was so deep in thought he almost tumbled into the cargo hold. I grabbed him and asked, 'Jambo, cap'n! What's on your mind?' That's when he asked how we could extend the *Persistence*'s range to compete with the larger, fleet-supported ships. It took a while, but what you see here is our solution—a diesel-electric combo that doubles our range. Now, no ocean's too far."

Grace raised her chin, glowing with pride. Tim didn't blame her—the system was impressive. As he studied the batteries and their coupling to the main propeller shafts, Peter chimed in, "What Grace isn't saying is it took more than three years and several dozen prototypes to make this work. There were times I thought it might be impossible. But every time, she'd grab my arms and say, 'Nonsense—just need to caress this invention a little more until it tells me what it needs.'"

Tim was stunned. Peter—the captain who seemed unshakable—had thought about giving up?

While Tim processed this, Grace added with a grin, "I always tell the cap'n, 'Where there's a will, there's a way.' And sure enough, we found our way with this system. We've still got a few tweaks to make—we're always learning, you know—but she's a beauty, isn't she?"

Tim nodded in awe, surprised by Grace's positive attitude. If he didn't know better, he'd think Grace had been the one to teach Peter the code!

"Well, Grace," Peter said, "we'll leave you to your latest modification. Thanks for taking a moment to meet Tim. And don't forget dinner—Jacques really outdid himself!"

"I can hardly wait, cap'n!" Grace said, rubbing the tools on her vest as if they were her stomach. With a giggle, she added, "And cap'n, make sure you show him my little present!"

"Dessert wouldn't be complete without it!" Peter said, and they shared a laugh.

"Nice meeting ya, Cap'n Tim. Fair winds and following seas to you—and when you don't get them, never give up." Grace gripped Tim's hand and gave it a vigorous shake.

Tim nodded and thanked her, then followed Peter back to the wardroom, hoping for some clarity on what he'd heard. As they entered, Peter peeked around the corner of his war chest to see if Jacques had dessert ready.

"When you're ready for dessert, just say the word, Captain," Jacques called from the galley.

Peter smiled. "Aye, aye, Jacques." Then, turning to Tim, he said, "That man has the best hearing of anyone I've ever met. Let's take a seat for a moment before dessert."

He motioned for Tim to reclaim his earlier chair. Tim paused to grab his notepad from the dinner table, and as he sat down Peter looked up.

"I bet you have a question or two," Peter said with a knowing smile.

"I sure do! Did she really say you were ready to give up on the battery system? *You*?"

"I'm not an engineer, and we had already spent a lot of money trying to make it work. I couldn't afford to sink more into it. But Grace—whom I trust with my life—convinced me she was close. She gave me a reason to believe in her and the system. So I gave her a deadline, Jacques kept her fed around the clock, and she rallied—working nights and weekends until she made it happen."

"So you didn't invent the system?" Tim asked, surprised.

"Not at all—Grace did. I just offered her the support she needed. In the end, she did two things: she invented the system, and she gave me the encouragement to keep believing." Peter smiled warmly.

"Why was Grace willing to work so hard for so long?" Tim asked, still curious.

Peter didn't hesitate. "Because she understood the 'why.' She knew that if the *Persistence* could double its range, we could do some remarkable things."

Tim cut him off. "Like, earn more money?"

Peter raised his eyebrows slightly. "Sure, we'd all make more money, but that wasn't the main driver." He stood and walked to the dining table, where Jacques had returned the fruit bowl—now missing a few pieces. Peter brought it back to the coffee table and set it down.

"Money wasn't what motivated Grace—it was this." Peter placed the wooden bowl on the table and waited.

"Huh? She did it for fruit? I'm not tracking."

"Take a closer look," Peter instructed.

As Tim leaned in, he realized the horizontal lines on the bowl weren't decorative—they were names. He turned the bowl, inspecting the inside and outside surfaces. Names were etched all over it. Curious, Tim removed a piece of fruit, then another, revealing more names beneath. He kept going until the bowl was empty, astonished by what he saw—there must have been a thousand names engraved in the wood.

Tim looked up at Peter, stunned.

Peter smiled, pride evident in his eyes. "That bowl was given to the crew of the *Persistence* by the chief of an African tribe we delivered food and medical supplies to," Peter explained. "Grace is originally from Tanzania. She knows firsthand how essential food and medical supplies are to the people of Africa. She's also a gifted engineer who wanted to be part of a team willing to sail around the world to help others. That's what drove her to build the diesel-electric system."

Tim sat silently, absorbing the deeper meaning.

"We keep the bowl filled with fruit because that's how the chief gave it to us. 'From this bowl may nourishment always flow for the crew of the *Persistence*.'" Peter paused as Tim admired the bowl, letting the significance sink in. "Now you understand the 'why' behind the propulsion system. But to fully appreciate it, you also need to understand the 'how.' That's what Action #6 is all about."

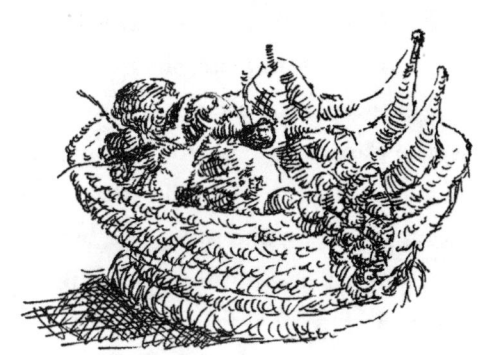

Tim set the bowl down and reached for his notepad, ready to capture his teacher's next lesson.

"Grace didn't create the system overnight," Peter said. "It took several prototypes before we had something we could take to sea. She kept experimenting, unsure of what would work or fail—it took over three years to get it right. She improvised, adapted, and overcame every obstacle." Peter emphasized the three verbs, ensuring their weight wasn't lost on Tim.

Tim picked up on the cue, writing the words in capital letters: IMPROVISE. ADAPT. OVERCOME.

"Every prototype came with new, unforeseen challenges," Peter continued. "Just when Grace thought she had it solved, another issue would arise. But each time, she adapted and found a way to overcome it. That's what you must do when faced with obstacles on your course—implement an action, adapt to the result, and keep going until you've conquered it.

"Be like a river—find your way over, under, around, or through. Keep flowing, and never stop trying. Your success will come from your ability to keep moving forward, no matter the obstacles."

"But even you said you were willing to give up—you were going to let an obstacle stop you," Tim said softly, careful not to sound disrespectful.

"Correct, and I'll explain shortly—it ties in to the last action. But you're right, I was questioning whether it could be done."

Before Tim could press further, Peter called out, "Jacques, we're ready for dessert!"

"Aye, aye, Captain. One minute to go," Jacques responded from the galley.

Peter tilted his head toward the table. "C'mon, I want to show you Grace's present—the one she gave me when she finished the system."

Tim grabbed his notebook and jumped to his feet, following Peter past the wardroom table to the port-side porthole. Peter flicked a switch, and a small directional light illuminated a sculpture made from cables, wires, nuts, bolts, and other odd bits.

At first, the sculpture looked like a jumble of scrap. Tim took a step back, trying to see it from a different angle.

"Is that a bird?" he asked.

"Very good. It's supposed to be a black egret—an African heron," Peter confirmed. "But Grace isn't exactly a sculptor. Can you tell what it's eating?"

Tim squinted, but it was obvious—a frog. Not just any frog, though. This one was ridiculously muscular. Tim chuckled, amused by its exaggerated physique. No frog had biceps like this one! Then he noticed something else: the egret had the frog's head in its mouth, but the frog was gripping the bird's neck with both hands. The bird's eyes, comically wide, looked like they were about to pop out of their sockets.

Tim laughed out loud. "Of course Grace made this! Look how ripped that frog is!"

As he stepped closer, he noticed four letters etched into the bronze base of the sculpture: **NEGU**.

"What does NEGU mean?" Tim asked.

Peter smiled. "It's Grace's way of spelling persistence: *Never Ever Give Up*."

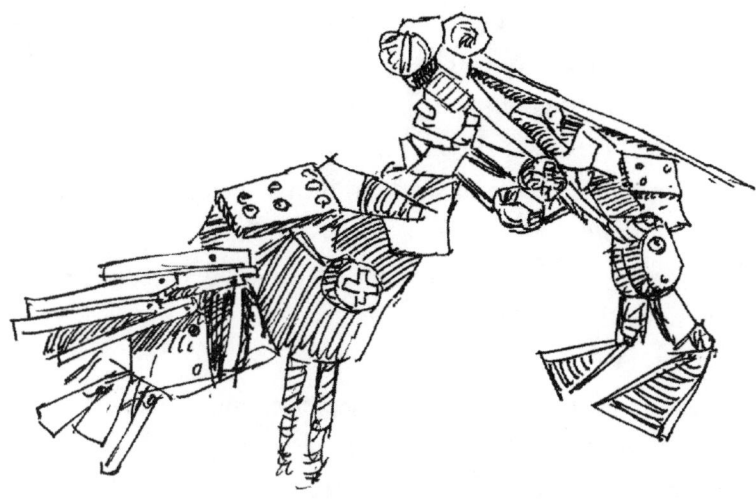

Grace's sculpture

They both burst out laughing.

Like clockwork, Jacques appeared, carrying two decadent desserts. The men quickly took their seats as Jacques placed bowls in front of them, each filled with succulent seasonal berries, slices of star fruit, and hand-churned vanilla ice cream. He left briefly, returning with a ceramic pitcher in one hand and a hand-blown glass bulb in the other.

Jacques drizzled buttery caramel over their desserts and finished with a sprinkle of sea salt from the glass bulb. Saying nothing, he returned to the galley. The savory dessert needed no explanation.

Both men grinned like kids in a candy store. Lifting his spoon, Peter said, "NEGU is exactly what the sixth action is all about. Be flexible, improvise, adapt, and keep trying new things until you overcome your obstacle. Got it?"

Peter beat Tim to the first bite. Tim hesitated, setting his spoon down, not wanting to forget his teacher's words. He circled the words *"Improvise, Adapt, Overcome,"* in his notebook and wrote *"Action #6"* above them. Below, he added, *"Be like the frog—Never Ever Give Up (NEGU)."*

They ate in companionable silence, racing to finish their dessert before the ice cream melted. From the galley, Jacques smiled as he heard the sound of spoons scraping ceramic bowls, the two men foraging for every last bit of caramel and cream.

When the scraping stopped, Jacques took it as his cue to clean up and prepare for breakfast. The *Persistence* would get underway early the next morning, and he liked to stay two meals ahead in case rough seas waited beyond the harbor.

As Jacques began clearing the table, Peter stood, extended his arms, and bowed slowly toward the chef. "Jacques, from start to finish, that was your finest meal yet. Thank you—we bow to you!"

Tim leapt to his feet, eager to match the gesture. "Thank you, grandmaster, for the most incredible meal I've ever eaten."

Jacques was touched by Tim's boyish sincerity. He understood why Peter was taking his time teaching this young captain the code. In Jacques's mind, the oceans needed more captains like Peter. With a subtle bow, Jacques replied, "It has been a pleasure, gentlemen. I'm honored you enjoyed my creations. You'll find refreshments on the teak table. Good night."

Tim paused at Jacques's parting words. Like Grace, the chef took full ownership of his work. Though their roles on the *Persistence* were entirely different, both approached their responsibilities as creators. Grace had built a complex hybrid propulsion system, and Jacques crafted masterpiece meals three times a day.

Tim marveled at how both took such pride in their work, always striving to improve. They were never satisfied—always searching for ways to be better. And then, it hit him like a rogue wave: Captain Peter hadn't just taught the code to future masters and commanders—he had taught it to his crew.

That meant the code was for anyone who wanted to excel at what they did.

Peter was pouring himself a glass of ice water when Tim, struck by his realization, nearly shouted, "The code isn't just for ship captains, is it?"

Peter turned slowly, smirking, and gestured for his pupil to continue.

"At first, when I saw Jacques working around the table, delivering those amazing meals, I thought, 'Wow, Captain Peter's really lucky to have a chef like him.' But then I met Grace, and she had the same attention to detail and the same can-do attitude. Both of them made a point of calling out their inventions, taking real pride in their work. I thought you got lucky with Jacques, but after meeting Grace, I realized you taught them the code."

Peter gave an approving nod. "I did. And bravo for noticing—you've got excellent powers of observation! And while I taught them the code, it's important to understand that they made it work for themselves. I can teach anyone the code, but I can't make them follow it. Some folks, like the barge captain you saw earlier today, have no interest in improving or learning. They're content just getting by. With experience, you'll learn to spot the difference between people who are satisfied with staying where they are and those, like Jacques or Grace—or you—who want to grow."

Peter took a sip of water, then gestured for Tim to join him on the ostrich-skin lounge chairs. As Tim scribbled notes, Peter continued, "The world needs both kinds of people. Not everyone wants to be a ship's captain, and frankly, not everyone should be. But for any captain to succeed, they need a crew with complementary talents. And here's the tricky part—you have to understand what you're good at and what you're not. You can't be great at everything."

Peter watched as Tim furiously jotted down notes.

"Tim, you need a crew that excels at what you don't. Leave your ego on the pier and accept that you won't always have the right answer. You'll need to trust your crew. And when you do . . ." Peter paused, a faint smile forming on his lips.

"What happens?" Tim asked, eager to know.

"They'll trust you. And here's the kicker—if you help them succeed, they'll help you do the same."

"It sure sounds simple when you say it like that. But that's not how they teach it in school," Tim replied. "There, it's all about managing hours and improving efficiency. They don't teach us how to trust or make those who work for us—"

"Tim," Peter interrupted, "don't ever think of people as possessions or servants. No one works *for* you—they work *with* you. Too many captains out there believe their crews are just there to follow orders. That mindset is a mistake. People treated like servants won't burn the midnight oil to solve problems—they'll spend their energy figuring out how to get off the ship. Never *for*—always *with*."

Tim sat upright, as if a teacher had just scolded him. "Got it—my apologies."

"Right. As you were saying, Tim."

"I was saying that in school, they don't teach us how to manage other . . ."

"Stop!" Peter barked, as if commanding his quartermaster. "People like Grace and Jacques don't want to be managed—they want to be led. They need a vision, a 'why' that inspires them, and they want to contribute to something bigger than themselves.

"To lead, you must let go. Don't hover over them or watch the clock. Arm them with what they need, encourage them, and support them. When they fall, help them up. When they succeed, praise them for the whole world to see. If they go off course, pull them aside quietly and discuss a course correction. But whatever you do, *don't try to manage them!*"

Peter paused for a moment, taking a long breath for effect, then asked, "Have I made myself clear?"

Tim answered sheepishly, "Yes, sir—crystal." He scribbled furiously, writing down the distinction between *manage* and *lead*. He circled and starred the words *for* and *manage* in his notes, then looked up at Peter, surprised at how quickly the captain's demeanor had changed when those words were used.

HOW TO
GET STARTED

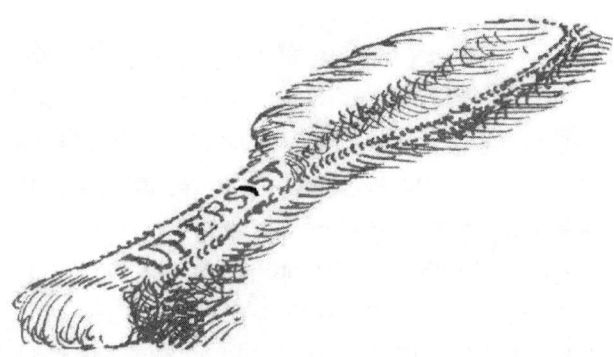

ACTION #6 | IMPROVISE

In the spring of 1997, I deployed with seven other SEALs to Sarajevo on a mission to capture a PIFWC—Person Indicted For a War Crime. At the time, military operations in Bosnia were labeled peacekeeping operations, with NATO countries responsible for maintaining peace in different regions. The frustrating part of the mission was that these PIFWCs were more than everyday thugs; they had committed unimaginable crimes against humanity. Yet, we weren't authorized to conduct direct-action missions to kill or capture them. Our rules of engagement limited us to setting up roadblocks to capture them alive so they could stand trial at The Hague.

At our command post, we had a poster listing seventy-seven PIFWCs, each assigned a number based on their importance. Our target was #3, wanted for crimes against humanity, including mass genocide. This man was responsible for orchestrating the deaths of over 60,000 men, women, and children. We didn't need a pep talk to understand the gravity of our mission.

During our prep, the Army colonel in charge informed me that the mission had caught the attention of a four-star general who wanted direct command and control over it. I told the colonel, "No problem, sir. We'll have Satcom radio with us—he can reach me anytime." I'll never forget his response: "Lew-Tenant Mills, that's not what the general has in mind. He wants to see the whites of this maggot's eyes—you need to send him a picture."

My boss, Colonel Stones (real name withheld), was a decorated Army Ranger with a laid-back Southern drawl and wasn't one to pull practical jokes. But I couldn't resist quipping, "So we're going to snap pictures of the bad guy, send the roll to be developed, and wait for the general's feedback?" A slight smile crept onto Colonel Stones's face as he replied, playing along with my sarcasm, "Yep, just like that—except for the film part. All the general needs is one good picture."

Before I could respond, the colonel reached under his desk and pulled out a black ruggedized case. He placed it on the desk with a thud and opened it to reveal what looked like a camera. It wasn't just any camera—it was a prototype of what we now know as a digital SLR.

"Before you touch it," Stones said, "you've got to sign for it—all $34,000 of it." I can still hear him adding with that easy drawl, "Now Lew-Tenant, don't go breakin' this camera. I'd hate to dock you a year's pay for it."

The camera and laptop presented a real challenge. Our mission required us to spend at least four days deep in the rugged mountains of Bosnia, close to hostile troops, while trying to photograph our target. We spent days preparing to use the camera and laptop tactically. From battery life to downloads and Satcom uploads, we tried to anticipate every possible way the technology could fail. Our planning helped us identify some critical limitations, like the short battery life and lack of durability.

Since Bosnia didn't exactly have a Best Buy for the forty laptop batteries we needed—most shops had been bombed out—and no waterproof bags to protect the equipment, we improvised. We figured out how to use our Satcom radio batteries to power the laptop and fashioned a one-off neoprene bag from an old wetsuit to protect the camera from the elements.

Even with all our preparation, we still missed a limitation that almost cost us the mission: the autofocus on the camera was painfully slow. Every time our target drove past, the camera couldn't focus fast enough to capture a clear picture of the PIFWC's car. I remember checking in with Colonel Stones and hearing the dreaded words, "Mission abort—pictures no good."

Our hearts sank. We *wanted* this guy.

We huddled, quickly hatched a plan, and radioed in: "Request twenty-four hours."

Colonel Stones came back flatly: "Interrogative—do you have a plan?"

"Affirmative, over," I responded.

The colonel granted us the extra time, and we got to work. That night, equipped with night-vision goggles, infrared lights, and a security perimeter, we set out to dig the perfect pothole. It took two nights to get it just right. Eight days later, we got the shot the general needed. Within a month, PIFWC #3 was in The Hague, where he would spend the rest of his life answering for the atrocities he had committed.

The point of this story isn't just that there was one less criminal on the streets of Bosnia—it's that there was one less criminal in the world because a small team refused to give up. Our relentless willingness to improvise made the mission a success.

I stress "team" because that's what it took to overcome the obstacles. It was the *team's* "never give up" mindset that propelled us forward, forcing us to improvise again and again until we succeeded.

This attitude isn't unique to the SEALs. Improvising is a habit, just like exercising or planning, and it takes time and practice to develop. It's not a talent you're born with—it's a mindset you create.

WARNING: This mindset isn't natural. Most people, when faced with an obstacle, see it as a limitation and stop. Improvising means more work, more failures, and trying new approaches. It's not normal—but neither is success.

Few people succeed in achieving their dreams. Those who do are the ones willing to take a different path. You won't find success by following the same road as everyone else.

My business partner and I learned this the hard way when we started Perfect Fitness. We sought out experts to teach us the "right way" to launch our brand on TV. Armed with this advice, we raised $1.5 million to create an infomercial to introduce our product, "BODYREV," to the market. Two and a half years later, we had learned $1,475,000 worth of ways *not* to launch a product. Down to our last $25,000, we knew we needed to improvise—and fast.

The hardest part was accepting that no matter how many messages we tried, we couldn't make BODYREV work on TV. Armed with more than two years of failures, we decided to create an entirely different product. We dusted off my design notebook and picked an idea I had invented as a platoon commander in SEAL Team TWO. With little cash and even less investor support (some investors told me to stop embarrassing myself and get a job), we launched the Perfect Pushup in the fall of 2006—four and a half years after I began my journey to build a fitness company.

Within two years, the improvised pivot paid off. We went from $500,000 in sales to over $60 million, gaining national recognition as the fourth-fastest-growing company in the U.S. in 2009. But just as we thought we had success by the reins, we had to improvise again. The 2008–09 economic downturn cost us our line of credit, and without bank support, we couldn't ship products to key customers. We were staring down bankruptcy and needed to act fast.

Twelve months later, we thought we had found a way to keep the company afloat—only to be forced to improvise a third time to avoid losing it entirely. We certainly didn't get everything right, and some of our actions didn't help. But we never gave up, relying on our ability to adapt and improvise until we found success.

Along the way, as we created what are now more than 40 patented products, I developed a framework I call the three "I's" of Improvise. Whenever you face a challenge, ask yourself: Do I need to **Improve**, **Innovate**, or **Invent** to succeed?

Let's take Perfect Fitness as an example of how to apply the three "I's." The simplest form of improvisation is **improving** something. Over half of our products are improvements, like the Perfect Pushup Stands. We enhanced the materials by adding nonslip rubberized grips on both the bottom and the handles, used better resins for a stronger base, and redesigned the structure for improved stability and safety. These kinds of improvements took weeks, not months or years, but they rarely lead to significant intellectual property protection, like utility patents.

If a simple improvement isn't enough, it's time to **innovate**. Our most popular products are innovations—products with a familiar reference point but containing a "surprise" that makes you say, "Whoa, I didn't see that coming." These innovations trigger a double take.

Examples include the Perfect Pushup, Perfect Pullup, and Perfect Ab Carver. The innovation—or surprise—in these products lies in their functionality: the pushup's rotating handles, the pullup bar's adjustable height, and the Ab Carver's internal spring. However, a key factor in the success of an innovation is understanding the "why" behind it. Innovating just to be different without solving a real problem is dangerous. Consumers can spot gimmicks a mile away. If your innovation feels like a "nice-to-have" instead of a "must-have," the product is doomed to a short life.

By far, the most challenging "I" is to **invent**. Today, the word *invent* is used loosely to describe any new idea. However, a true invention introduces something entirely new with no prior reference point—like the Segway (a two-wheeled, gyro-balancing people mover) or, in my case, the BODYREV, a rotating weight system. Inventions take significant time to develop, but even more time to educate people on how to use them. (I tell folks to budget three times the length of development for education.)

At Perfect Fitness, about 10% of our time was spent working on inventions. Often, we pursue inventions knowing they may never make it to market—only to discover insights along the way that improve other products. Great teams embrace the process of invention, but they also value the impact of improvements and innovations.

The scary part of improvising is that you don't know how things will turn out. And that's okay—nobody does. But if you don't try, the result is guaranteed: nothing.

One of the best pieces of advice I ever received came from my second commanding officer at SEAL Delivery Team TWO. Just before I deployed on a special project mission, he pulled me aside and said, "Lieutenant Mills, always remember—no matter what happens, make a decision and take action. If it's the wrong decision, you'll know quickly, and you can make a better one. But whatever you do, *make a decision.* Not taking action kills people."

I've never forgotten those words—or that officer. He was a remarkable leader.

To improvise is to **take action**. You won't know if it's the right action until you follow the path of your decision. If it turns out to be wrong, don't get stuck in regret—smile and say, "Okay, I just learned another way *not* to do it," and move on.

I've failed more times than I've succeeded, but each failure has been a building block for success. Every success I've had began with improvising.

The key to building an improvising mindset is to create a habit of asking, "Is there a better way to do this?" This question, asked consistently, will guide you toward success. Don't wait until you're cornered to ask it. Ask it throughout your journey—whether you're reading a news story, watching a sports game, sitting in a classroom, or scrolling through the internet.

Building an improvising mindset starts *now*, not when you're stuck. Like any skill, the more you practice, the better you'll get.

I'm confident that no matter what you focus on, you can find a better way. Lots of people have good ideas—but what will set you apart is your willingness to act on them.

When an obstacle stands between you and your goal, smile. Know that the obstacle is there to stop the ones who lack the courage or willingness to improvise. You are not like everyone else. You welcome obstacles, because overcoming them makes you stronger.

And the best part? You're ready, because you know the secret: **improvise**!

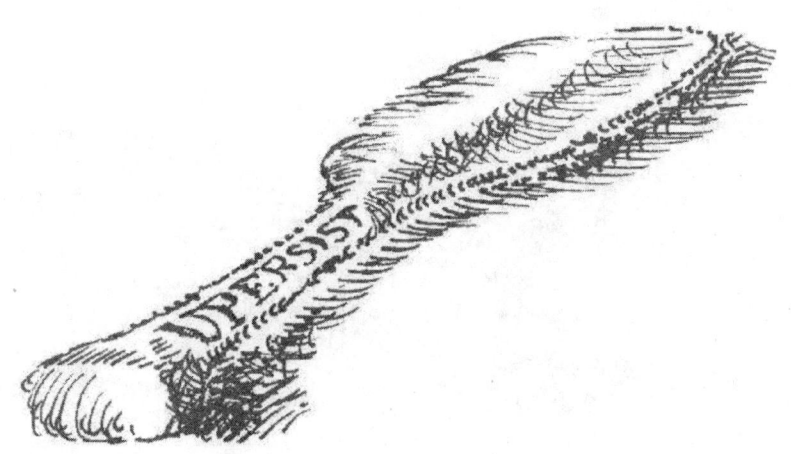

ACTION #7
Seek Expert Advice

The senior skipper studied his pupil as if inspecting his vessel before setting sail. Tim met his gaze cautiously, still mindful of how quickly Peter's demeanor had shifted during their conversation about leading versus managing. It was clear that the master and commander was deeply passionate about the code—and even more passionate about helping others achieve their dreams. Tim understood now that Peter wasn't being harsh for the sake of it; he just wanted his lessons to stick. Tim leaned forward, eager to hear the next action. He was ready for Action #7.

The skipper noticed the shift in Tim's posture. The more time he spent with Tim, the more certain he became that this young captain had the courage to follow the code. Peter cleared his throat.

"Now, that key difference between 'manage' and 'lead' ties directly to the final two actions of the Code. I'll break it down to make it easy, but the essence of Action #7 comes down to three things." Peter held up three fingers. "First, get comfortable with the fact that you'll never be great at everything. Second, understand your talents—know what you're good at and what you're not. And third, find people who excel at what you don't do well.

"Remember when I said to leave your ego on the pier? It's not easy at first—you're wearing the captain's stripes, and you feel like you need to have all the answers. But you don't, and the sooner you accept that, the faster you'll learn from those who *do*. If you catch yourself second-guessing, I want you to remember this: *If you're thinking twice, seek expert advice.*"

Peter paused and locked eyes with Tim.

Tim repeated it softly and slowly.

Leave your ego at the pier

"Grace didn't know the first thing about batteries," Peter went on. "She thought a lot more than twice, so she reached out to experts worldwide to figure out how to combine them with the diesel engines she understood. Same with Jacques—when I met him, he couldn't prepare seafood to save his life. That Japanese master and commander—the one who gave me the river rock—connected him with a sushi chef, who taught him a whole new skill set. And remember why I'm here? To seek advice on new propellers."

Peter leaned in. "The point is, once you recognize a weakness or try something new—or if you're 'thinking twice'—find people who've already done it. They have the knowledge you don't. That's what the seventh action is about: Seek expert advice."

The younger captain nodded again at the master and commander's advice. As he exhaled, a half-chuckle escaped, prompting his teacher to ask, "What's so amusing, Tim?"

"I just realized I'm already practicing Action #7 by talking to you," Tim said with a grin.

"Well, you've been an excellent student so far! It's a simple, logical approach, but you'd be surprised how many captains avoid it. They convince themselves 'I'm good enough,' or 'I know enough,' or 'I'll figure it out.' A whole list of excuses stops them from asking for help. The seafloor is littered with ships—and captains—who decided not to seek expert advice."

Peter let the words hang for a moment, then shifted into a commanding tone. "Captain Tim, be the captain who admits what he knows—and what he doesn't—and seeks expert advice. Have I made myself clear?"

Tim sat bolt upright, his gaze locked on Peter. Nearly saluting, he responded with confidence, "When I'm thinking twice, I will seek expert advice!"

Peter narrowed his eyes, studying Tim's response. After a few moments, he gave a small, approving nod.

"We've got one action left, my friend. Then comes the real test," Peter said, his voice measured.

For the first time in hours, Tim felt another wave of unease. Shifting in his seat, he asked nervously, "Uh . . . anything I should know before we get to the next action? You know, just to be prepared?"

"No need to worry," Peter said casually, eyeing Tim with a hint of mischief. "It's just your final exam for understanding the code."

"Final exam?" Tim blurted out, his eyes widening. "You never said anything about a final exam!"

HOW TO
GET STARTED

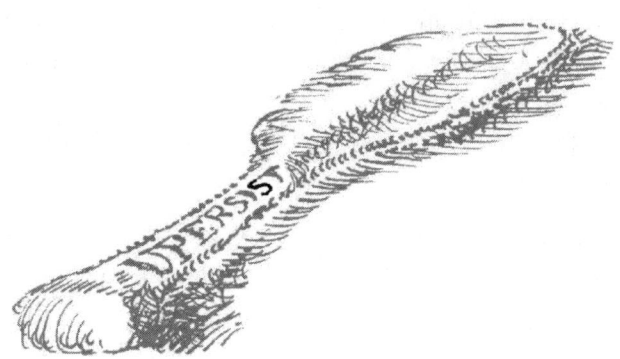

ACTION #7 | SEEK EXPERT ADVICE

There's nothing complicated about Action #7—it's exactly what it sounds like: seek expert advice. This was always our first step as SEALs after receiving a mission assignment, and it was the first thing we did when deciding what product to launch at Perfect Fitness. The premise is simple: learn from those who've already traveled the path you're on.

If you search carefully and ask thoughtfully, you'll usually find someone willing to share advice that can increase your chances of success. Depending on your goal and the value of their insights, you may need to offer more than a thank-you note—compensation, such as money or stock, might be required. But the right expert can save you hundreds, if not thousands, of hours in trial and error, getting you closer to your goal faster.

The real challenge with Action #7 lies within—it's your ego. We like to believe we know it all. We're often bold in our ideas but hesitant to seek outside guidance. Yet the news is full of people who failed spectacularly because they didn't ask for advice from someone who had already faced similar challenges. Seeking an expert is no different from asking a teacher for help with a difficult homework problem. Depending on the size and ambition of your goal, you might need advice from several experts to map out your path to success. The sooner you accept that you don't—and won't—know everything, the sooner you'll move closer to achieving your dreams.

In the SEALs, junior officers (JOs) have only a brief window to earn the respect of their platoon mates—a critical milestone in establishing themselves as leaders others would trust in combat. Arriving with a college degree and a BUD/S certificate doesn't earn respect; it merely gets you in the door. What truly matters is your ability to ask for advice, even from those who technically report to you. These teammates have far more experience than you as a SEAL, and their insights are invaluable.

This is one of the great paradoxes of leadership: the person in charge often has the least experience.

A JO's SEAL career can be cut short if they don't acknowledge how little they know. I was no different. Eager to earn the respect of veteran SEALs, I was excited to dive into the work. Thankfully, two warrant officers took me and another JO under their wing, teaching us the value of learning from others. These officers became our experts, showing us everything we needed to survive and succeed while operating a classified combat mini-submersible, the SEAL Delivery Vehicle. Without them, my SEAL career would have taken a very different path. Their teachings saved my life—and others'—more times than I care to count.

I admit I didn't always seek their advice, though. There were times I believed I had mastered what they taught me, and every time arrogance crept in I made mistakes. They often reminded us: *"Arrogance kills."* SEAL teams, despite their reputation, are not immune to this mindset. History is filled with instances where arrogance—often in the form of an officer's unwillingness to seek advice—led to injury or death.

While this might be an extreme example of the consequences of not seeking expert advice, the principle holds: You will never know it all. Use experts to help you excel. Every time I set a new goal, I follow three steps:

1. **Define the goal:** Make it as measurable as possible.
2. **Define my "why":** Why is this goal worth pursuing? Why is it worth my time and energy?
3. **Identify who can help:** Determine who can assist me in getting started.

Be ready to seek out different types of experts along your journey. Some will help you get started, others will help you when you hit roadblocks, and a few will guide you across the finish line. I categorize experts using the acronym **S.E.T.**—*Strategic, Emergency, and Tactical*—as in, *"Get SET!"* like you're at the starting line of a race. (And you are—because every time you leave your comfort zone, you're starting a new race.)

Some experts may fit multiple roles, like a parent who serves as both a Strategic and Emergency expert. But as your goals grow bigger and bolder, so will your need for a diverse "S.E.T." team.

When I started Perfect Fitness, I sought out experts in operations, finance, industrial design, marketing, infomercials, sales, e-commerce, HR, banking, accounting, and legal issues. I can't stress this enough: you'll need help, so get comfortable asking for it. Your experts will either be your greatest asset or your biggest liability. The quality of your experts directly affects your success, and the sooner you embrace this, the faster you'll reach your goals. *Put your pride aside—seek expert advice!*

People often ask how I invented the Perfect Pushup. The short answer? I invented it with about 25 other people. Sure, I had the initial idea, but an idea isn't worth the napkin it's sketched on without experts helping to make it real. Some of these experts may even join you on your journey—and that's what the eighth and final action is all about.

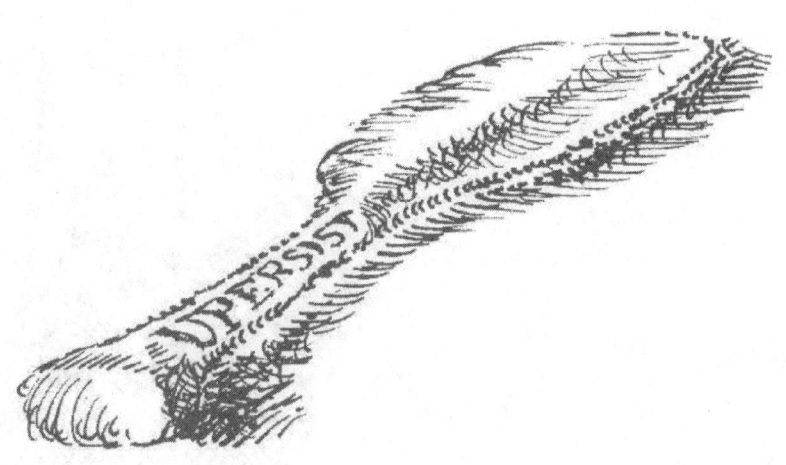

ACTION #8
Team Up

The master laughed heartily. "Of course there's a final exam! How else will you really learn the code?" Peter grinned as Tim anxiously flipped through his notes, trying in vain to cram, and gave the young captain a reassuring smile. "Relax, Tim. It's a take-home exam. Pencil down so you can focus on the last action."

Tim exhaled deeply, placed his pencil across his notepad, and leaned back. "I'm all ears, skipper."

"Good. Let's start with the basics." Peter leaned forward with his

elbows resting just above his knees. "Remember when we talked about how some courses in life require more effort than others?"

Tim nodded. "Yes, you said no two courses are alike—some will be easier, some harder."

"Exactly right," Peter replied. "Action #8 is about those courses you choose that truly challenge you—the kind that scare the hell out of you and make you wonder, *How on earth am I going to pull this off?*"

Peter's calm assurance made it sound like it was only a matter of time before Tim would take on one of those daunting paths. That thought alone made Tim shift uneasily in his seat.

"The harder the course, the more rewarding it will be. I promise, Tim. But you won't be able to do it alone. As your confidence grows, you'll take on bigger challenges—until one day, you'll choose a course that's *way* outside your comfort zone. Like when I decided to steam across an entire ocean. I had no clue how to do it. Do you know how I figured it out?"

This time Peter waited patiently for an answer. Tim thought before blurting out, "You used Action #7!"

Peter beamed with pride, pleased at how quickly his student was absorbing the code. "Exactly! I started by asking people who had already done it. And do you know what they all told me?"

Tim hesitated, the weight of getting the last answer right making him even more careful. He didn't want to break his streak. "That . . . you couldn't do it alone?"

"Yes! That's exactly what they told me," Peter said, his excitement growing. He could tell the code was clicking for Tim, and he wanted to encourage him as much as possible—this might be their last conversation, though he sincerely hoped it wouldn't be. "Every one of those old captains said, 'Son, don't be foolish. Crossing an ocean takes more than one person—and not just any person. You need a crew that's both competent and confident.'"

Peter's voice softened as he reflected. "That advice led me to Grace and Jacques. And thank goodness I listened. I already knew the code, but those old salts reminded me of the importance of Action #8: I needed to team up with people who were great at things I wasn't. That's the key—after seeking expert advice, you need to build a team that complements what you've learned."

Peter leaned in, eyes twinkling. "Now, Tim, how are you going to attract the right people for your journey? That's connected to Action #1."

"I'm going to find teammates who are as inspired by my 'why' as I am! Wait, that means I'll be repeating the code, but this time with more people following along! I get it—it's a cycle. Once I accomplish something, I put the code to work again, but on a bigger course. And as the course demands more people, the code applies to a team. But it all starts with figuring out the 'why.'"

Tim's words came faster as the logic of the code clicked. "And with a team, you figure out the way together—which means you cover more ground faster. You can achieve so much more if everyone believes in the 'why'!"

He jumped to his feet, made a fist with his right hand, and smacked it into his left palm, letting out a yelp of delight—he finally understood the code. He saw how actions connected and could be scaled. His mind raced with the possibilities. Captain Tim would never be the same. He was already thinking differently. He was inspired to dream big.

As he bounced around the wardroom, he noticed more artifacts of various shapes and sizes. He figured each one marked a dream Captain Peter had navigated. He couldn't wait to start his own journey and collect mementos of his own—to build his own war chest.

The master and commander smiled, proud to see the lights turn on in his pupil's mind. This moment never got old—helping the next generation see their potential. He wished he could stand beside each student he'd taught the code, cheering them on through stumbles, encouraging them when the elements worked against them, and celebrating their successes. But the code's premise was that every student had to discover their own course. He couldn't do it for them, just as he couldn't steer their ships—it was up to them.

Instead, he'd created a keepsake for each student he mentored. Now was the time to present Tim with his first master-and-commander memento.

Lost in thought, Tim paced back and forth, silently repeating the code, unaware that Peter had opened the bottom shelf of his war chest and retrieved a miniature paddle.

Peter cleared his throat and stood across from Tim, who still had his back turned. "Tim, the time has come, my friend."

Tim knew the evening would end soon, though it was hard to hear. His heart sank slightly. He'd never experienced anything like this—it had been life-changing.

When he turned, Peter stood with arms outstretched, holding a beautiful small paddle. The wood glistened under the wardroom light.

"Tim, this is for you. It's more than just a memento of our evening—it's a checklist and a constant reminder of what it takes to be a master and commander," Peter said proudly, offering the gift.

Tim's mouth hung open. The evening had already surpassed anything he could have imagined. But this paddle—it wasn't just a paddle. It was a work of art and a tool for inspiration all at once.

A memento

"Go ahead, read it," Peter encouraged.

Still speechless, Tim carefully took the paddle, inspecting it from handle to blade tip. Letters and words were carved along the handle, stem, and blade. On the handle, the word "U-PERSIST" ran down the stem. On the blade was the quotation from the compass at Peter's helm:

> *Nothing in the world can take the place of persistence. Talent will not; nothing is more common than unsuccessful men with talent. Genius will not; unrewarded genius is almost a proverb. Education will not; the world is full of educated derelicts. Persistence and determination alone are omnipotent. The slogan "Press On" has solved and always will solve the problems of the human race.*

At the very bottom, Tim noticed four letters—N E G U—clearly carved by another hand. He smiled. Those letters had Grace's touch for sure.

Peter cleared his throat. He always got a bit emotional when handing over a paddle to one of his students. It was his way of being there for them, especially when they faced challenges alone. He hoped it would inspire Tim when doubt crept in, whispering to keep going when the winds and waves felt overwhelming.

"Tim," Peter began with a warm smile, "it is with great honor that I present you with this master and commander paddle. It symbolizes the earliest form of propulsion. Long before there were propellers, sails, steam engines, or electric motors—there was the paddle. So, I thought it fitting that the code and its meaning be inscribed on this symbol of navigation."

Peter pointed to the quote on the blade, eyes twinkling. "And don't forget Grace's definition: *Never, Ever Give Up.*"

Tim nodded enthusiastically but paused when his gaze returned to the letters carved from the handle to the stem. He looked puzzled, and Peter noticed.

"Those letters," Peter explained, "are the first initials of the eight actions of the code. They guide you on how to navigate any course: U-PERSIST."

Tim's eyes widened with recognition. For the first time, the actions clicked into place. He began to say them aloud:

"U — Understand. P — Plan. E — Exercise. R — Recognize. S — Survey. I — Improvise. S — Seek. T — Team up."

"It's brilliant!" Tim exclaimed, grinning from ear to ear. "I wondered how I'd remember all eight actions!"

"There's beauty in simplicity, my friend," Peter said. "The code is simple, and I've framed it so it's easy to remember. But using it—that's up to you, and you alone. I hope this paddle reminds you that you are limited by only two things: your ability to dream and the courage to pursue those dreams. There's an amazing world waiting for you beyond this harbor."

Peter gestured toward the bow of the *Persistence*, pointed toward the bay of Hardwork Harbor. "You have the boat and the brains to explore the world. Now, all that's left is to find a course—and have the courage to follow it."

Peter paused for emphasis, moving closer to Tim. "Tim, the wind, waves, and water can either work for you or against you—they'll kill you or carry you. It's all in how you respond to their forces. Sometimes they'll feel like nothing but obstacles. When they do, smile and learn, because the obstacle *is* your course. Never stop learning, especially when facing adversity. Remember, your brain is only as good as the inputs you give it. Fill it with new knowledge and ideas—things that help you dream up new courses to conquer. Your life is *up to you!*"

As Peter spoke the final words, he grabbed Tim's biceps firmly and stared into his eyes, making sure the message landed. Tim had to understand: the choices, the courses, the journey—everything—was up to him.

The young captain glanced down at the paddle, though his eyes were unfocused. A few tears escaped—tears of joy, sadness, and gratitude for what Peter had given him. No one had taken such a personal interest in him since he'd left home for school. The master and commander had filled him with hope, encouragement, and inspiration, leaving him ready to conquer the world.

But as the lump in his throat grew, Tim realized he had no idea how to thank this remarkable teacher. All he could do was bow his head, silently trying to hold back the overwhelming emotion.

Tim mustered a muffled "thank you" and wiped away his tears as the paddle and its inscribed words came back into focus. Peter smiled proudly at his new star student and said, "Turn the paddle over. There's a cheat sheet on the back—and one more quote to make sure you never forget what the code is all about."

Tim flipped the paddle and read the inscription on the back of the blade:

Understand the why, and you'll figure out the way
Plan in three dimensions
Exercise to execute
Recognize your reason to believe
Survey your habits

Improvise to overcome
Seek expert advice
Team up

"Before the gates of excellence, the high gods have placed sweat."

Peter could feel Tim's gratitude without needing to hear a word. His student's expression was enough. With a grin, Peter pulled him into a big bear hug and said, "From here on out, Captain, face forward and always point your bow out to sea. It's not about where you've been—it's about where you're going."

Tim gave a silent nod, collecting himself as he prepared to go ashore. Just as he thought the lesson was over, Peter left him with one last piece of advice. "Speaking of 'going' places," Peter said with a sly grin, "if you ever feel inspired to leave the harbor, may I suggest charting a course to the Big Island in the BYIs—seek the Harbor Master."

Tim's thoughts raced, emotions swirling at the sound of yet another cryptic riddle from his teacher. He wasn't ready to leave. He wanted to ask more questions, to stay in the moment just a little longer. But deep down, he knew it was time.

Peter, seeing the hesitation, gave him a knowing smile and said, "Time to go ashore, shipmate!"

As the two captains walked down the gangplank of the *Persistence*, Tim's mind swirled with questions. "Who's the Harbor Master? Where are the BYIs? And most importantly, what will I learn there?" The young skipper was so lost in thought that he didn't notice Captain Peter had stopped just before stepping off the gangplank.

Clutching his notebook in one hand and the paddle in the other, Tim realized he was suddenly alone. Startled, he turned back to get one last look at the remarkable vessel—and its captain.

Peter stood tall on the final rung of the gangplank, pride radiating from his stance. With the precision of a seasoned sailor, the master and commander gave a crisp right-handed salute. His voice, now that of a captain delivering a command, was firm and resolute:

"Full speed ahead, captain. Your course awaits. Work hard, have fun, and never, ever give up. And always remember where you came from. Your life is *up to you!*"

Tim didn't fall asleep until well after four bells sounded on his ship's chronometer. His mind was racing, processing every moment of the evening aboard the *Persistence*. His thoughts bounced from reciting the eight actions of the Master and Commander Code to recalling his conversations with Grace, Jacques, and, of course, Captain Peter.

He kept replaying the meal onboard—the flavors, the experience. He wished he could savor it all over again. As he mentally revisited each bite of Jacques's culinary creations, his thoughts drifted to the artifacts Peter had collected. Were they connected to Peter's cryptic words about the Big Island, the BYIs, and the Harbor Master? Tim even found himself imagining where he might display the mementos he hoped to collect from his own adventures. At one point, as he tossed and turned in his bunk, he thought about measuring a space in his cramped wardroom to build a war chest of his own.

Finally, as drowsiness crept over him, Tim's last thoughts were of the next course he would set for himself.

A long, resonant blast from a departing ship's whistle jolted Tim awake. It took him a minute to orient himself. He'd slept so soundly that, for a moment, he wasn't sure where he was. Had his evening with Captain Peter really happened? Or had it all been a dream?

A pit formed in his stomach. What if the *Persistence* and everything that had happened aboard were just a figment of his imagination? Panic rising, Tim scrambled to the nearest porthole, pressing his face against the glass to get a view of the mooring. He squinted into the morning sun reflecting off the calm water—and his heart sank. The mooring was empty.

The *Persistence* was gone.

A wave of doubt hit him. Had he imagined it all? Then he remembered the paddle. If he could find it, he'd know it was real. He tore through his quarters, searching frantically—no paddle. The knot in his stomach tightened as he raced through the galley and miniature wardroom—still nothing. Desperation set in.

Then, as he stormed onto the bridge, his eyes locked on it. There, perched above the compass with its handle facing the bulkhead, was the master and commander paddle.

Tim let out a relieved laugh, shaking his head at himself. Of course it had been real. He picked up the paddle and inspected it closely, ensuring every word of the engraved code was still intact. Satisfied, he searched for some heavy-duty tape. Until he could craft proper brass brackets, the tape would have to do.

He secured the paddle above the compass, wanting it prominently displayed on the bridge—a constant reminder of the code and Captain Peter's lessons. As he finished taping it into place, a sudden radio transmission interrupted his thoughts.

"Calling Captain Tim, Calling Captain Tim, this is Captain Bill. Please report your status and your Echo Tango Alpha, over."

The radio transmission hit Tim like a bucket of ice water. He nearly dropped the paddle as he scrambled to collect his thoughts and respond. In all the excitement, he'd completely forgotten that he needed to steam back across the bay today. The pit in his stomach returned as he hastily finished taping the paddle above the compass.

Grabbing the radio mic, he replied with little enthusiasm: "Cap'n Bill, this is Cap'n Tim. I read you loud and clear—will be underway shortly." He quickly ran an estimated time of arrival in his head and added, "Expect to arrive at 1600 hours . . . *BREAK* . . . belay my last—Echo Tango Alpha—1600 hours—over."

Captain Bill responded almost immediately: "Roger, copy all, Captain Tim—I'll be monitoring Channel 72 if you need assistance. Transit safely. Captain Bill out."

Tim sighed. As much as he wanted to stay on the bridge and daydream about the previous night, there was no time. He'd overslept, and there was a lot to do if he had any chance of making it home by 1600 hours.

He checked out with the repair crew, verified that all cargo had been properly off-loaded, and went through his normal pre-departure checklist. With everything squared away, Tim prepared to steam across the bay.

The pier-side line handlers shouted in perfect unison, "All clear, skipper!" Tim responded with one prolonged blast of the ship's whistle, signaling his departure. He set a reciprocal course back to the south side of Hardwork Harbor. But this time, there was no nervousness in his belly. He drew strength from Captain Peter's words, replaying part of their conversation in his mind.

He could hear the master and commander's voice clearly: *"Tim, my attitude is, if you don't run aground from time to time, you're not trying hard enough. What matters is that you understand why you ran aground."*

The young skipper grinned, knowing exactly why—and where—he'd run aground two days ago. With a chuckle, he said aloud, "Not this time, Buoys 15 and 17—you two are on my chart now."

The return journey went smoothly, and Tim arrived fifteen minutes ahead of his estimated time. He had been so focused on navigating that he didn't even notice the snide remarks crackling over the radio from Ted and his little fleet of so-called friends.

Tim returned a different captain, and Ted sensed it immediately from the way Tim responded on the pier.

"Hey, Captain Sandbar, how was the trip across the bay?" Ted called out, earning chuckles from the other young captains hanging nearby.

Tim smiled, standing a little taller as he turned to Ted and replied, "It was fantastic! Thanks for asking—can't wait to do it again."

The energy in Tim's voice startled Ted, and even Captain Bill, standing nearby to debrief Tim, raised an eyebrow in approval. Before Ted could come up with a retort, Tim turned to the senior captain and said, "Cap'n Bill, I'd like to share what I learned. Where would you like to conduct the debrief, sir?"

The elder skipper grinned. "Sounds good to me, skipper. How about we do the debrief on the quarterdeck with the other captains running the course tomorrow?"

"Aye, aye, Cap'n," Tim responded with confidence, turning away and leaving Ted and his followers speechless on the dock.

Ted hadn't expected this. Normally, Tim would drop his head, roll his shoulders, and retreat after one of Ted's jabs. But now Tim seemed taller, more composed. The usual insecurity was gone, replaced by a quiet confidence.

Still, Ted defaulted to what he knew best: insults. Just loud enough for Tim to hear, he quipped, "Look, fellas, there goes the first one in our class to run his ship aground. Maybe he should go back to Navigation 101!"

His friends chuckled, though not as heartily as Ted had expected. Something about Tim's demeanor made the joke fall flat.

And as Ted kept trying to undermine Tim with sarcasm and backhanded remarks, Tim quietly got to work. Over the following weeks, Tim earned a spot on the cargo fleet's weekly rotation, navigating to the north side of Hardwork Harbor. With every new course, his skills grew. Whenever his schedule allowed, Tim stopped by Cap'n Jack's Clam Shack, always secretly hoping to find Captain Peter seated at the helmsman's table.

As the weeks turned into months, Tim charted new routes and visited every port in and around Hardwork Harbor. He kept meticulous logs of each journey, documenting lessons learned and insights gained. Bit by bit, he made improvements to his ship—widening the cargo bays to handle bigger loads, installing ramps to carry a variety of goods. But it wasn't any single modification that made the biggest impact.

What changed everything was the confidence he gained from proving one of his ideas worked. That small but pivotal success reshaped his mindset, transforming the way he approached every future challenge.

Tim hadn't run aground since that first course north through Hardwork Harbor, but the experience lingered. It had scared him deeply. Every time he took his ship out, the thought of running aground haunted him, creeping into his dreams and making him throttle back when he could have sailed faster. The fear held him captive, limiting his ambitions. As much as he wanted to be like Captain Peter and explore beyond the harbor, he couldn't shake the anxiety of getting stuck again.

Then one sleepless night, as he prepared for yet another course across the harbor, a new idea struck him: *If I can't get rid of the fear of running aground, why not create something to shield myself from it?*

That night, wild ideas bounced through his mind—everything from extending metal sensors under the bow to affixing bulldozer tracks to the bottom of his ship to roll over sandbars. What started as a late-night thought experiment turned into several nights of tinkering and sketching, followed by weekends spent trying to design a real solution to his fear.

Eventually, Tim landed on a simple, practical idea: build a metal cage around the propeller. After all, it was the damaged propeller that had stranded him the first time. If he could prevent it from breaking, his ship could pull free from most obstacles. Suddenly, Tim's fear didn't seem as paralyzing. In fact, the idea of running aground became exciting—it was a challenge to solve, not a disaster to fear.

With the cage installed, Tim set out deliberately searching for a sandbar to test his solution. As he sailed, he thought of Captain Peter's painting—the one of the smiling captain heading into a storm. Less than a year after meeting the master and commander, Tim was ready to

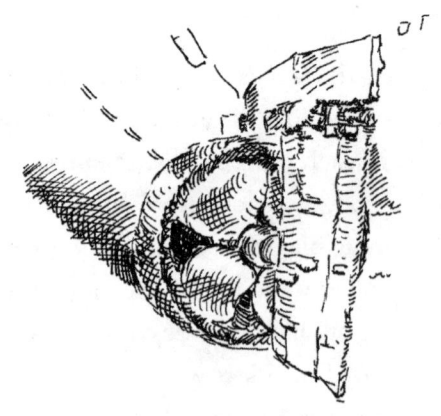

Captain Tim's solution

find his own "storm" to conquer. And he knew exactly where to face it: between buoys 15 and 17.

Tim throttled back, spun the helm to right full rudder, and eased his ship onto the sandbar. The hull ground to a halt on the sandy bottom, but Tim didn't panic. Instead, he smiled.

"What a difference an attitude makes," he said aloud, glancing at the paddle from Captain Peter that hung above the compass. Taking a deep breath, Tim shifted the engine into reverse. For a few tense seconds, nothing happened. His heart pounded in his chest—but then, he felt it. The propeller churned the water, and the stern sank slightly as the cage bumped against the edge of the sandbar.

With the propeller protected, it delivered just enough thrust to pull the ship free. Inch by inch, the boat backed off the sandbar, reversing course until it floated once more in open water.

Tim held his breath the whole time, and when the ship finally moved, he erupted in celebration: "Yes! Yes! Yes! It worked! I did it!"

On the bridge, Tim broke into a spontaneous dance, grinning ear to ear. He throttled back the engine, turned his ship toward the harbor, and headed home—victorious.

From that moment on, Tim's pace of ship modifications quickened. He experimented constantly—some ideas worked, and many didn't, but none of the failures slowed him down. The thrill was in the trying. As he spent more time dreaming up improvements for his ship, tracking work hours became irrelevant to him. Captain Tim no longer felt pressured to clock in at 8 a.m. or count down to 5 p.m. Instead, he woke early, eager to get to his ship, and stayed late into the night, completely absorbed in his work. Time didn't matter—it was about passion, not a schedule. His mindset shifted from the common fleet mantra of "work to live" to Captain Peter's philosophy: *"Live to work."*

The confidence Tim gained from overcoming his fear of running aground sparked even bigger dreams. He was ready to set a new course—this time, one that would take him beyond the boundaries of Hardwork Harbor.

Tim's course out of the bay began the moment he answered Captain Peter's question about what he was willing to give up to follow his own dreams. His confidence and courage to leave Hardwork Harbor didn't grow overnight. It took over two years of planning after that evening on the *Persistence* with Captain Peter, learning the Master and Commander Code. Tim spent countless late nights and weekends wrestling with the obstacles that held him back from pursuing his own course. He knew that if he did only what the fleet required, he would never leave the bay.

To achieve the freedom to follow his path, he realized he had to go beyond the expectations of his friends, family, and senior captains. If he wanted an extraordinary life, extraordinary sacrifices were the price. He had to work harder, think differently, and be unafraid to stand out among the other captains. Tim embraced failure as part of the journey. He grew comfortable confronting his fears—learning it was okay to be afraid, but also understanding that it was up to him not to let fear control his course.

Looking back, Tim hadn't realized it then, but every step since meeting Captain Peter had set him on the path of a master and commander. Often, he'd fall asleep imagining life as one, seeing it as a destination. What he didn't realize was that he'd already become a master and commander the moment he committed to trying a little harder and working a little longer each day. Captain Peter hadn't told Tim that following your own course—and living by the code—makes you your own master and commander.

There was, however, one small detail Captain Peter hadn't shared, which delayed Tim's departure by a day. The morning Tim informed Captain Bill of his plan to set sail, the elder captain asked, "Do you have your courses plotted, Tim?"

Tim replied proudly, "Yes, sir, plotted and double-checked."

Bill smiled. "Good—so, where are you headed, captain?"

Without hesitation, Tim answered with excitement, "To the Big Island of the BYIs."

The senior sailor nodded with a knowing smile. "I'm sorry, Tim, but you can't leave today."

Tim blinked, incredulous. "Why not? I'm ready!"

"I know you are. But your ship isn't," Bill replied, a glimmer of humor in his eye. "You need a name for your ship—it's international maritime law." Chuckling, he added, "One more day won't keep you from your course, Tim. Name your ship proudly. And may you have fair winds and following seas. When you don't, may you never, ever give up."

Tim stood, stunned. Before he could respond, Captain Bill gave him a grin. "Oh, and one more thing. When you get to the Big Island, give the Harbor Master a salute from me."

Tim's eyes nearly popped out of his head at Captain Bill's parting request. He sounded just like Captain Peter! Captain Bill—the one who had been there when Tim first ran aground, the one always offering help and asking what Tim had learned from his crossings—was he a master and commander too? And how did he know about the Harbor Master on the Big Island of the BYIs?

These thoughts swirled in Tim's mind as he spent the rest of the day deciding what to name his ship. Pacing the bridge, he glanced repeatedly at the paddle Captain Peter had given him, reflecting on all it symbolized. As the sun dipped low, casting its last rays through the trees and ships along the shoreline, inspiration struck.

That evening, Tim visited a woodworker friend and helped carve the name into three planks of teak. Once finished, he used brass screws to affix two planks to the port and starboard sides of the bridge and the third to the transom. Now, at last, Tim was ready to leave the bay and follow the course he'd charted to the BYIs.

The next morning, Tim rose early, double-checking everything on his ship to ensure it was ready for the journey. As he was finishing up, Captain Bill arrived with a few senior captains to see him off. They helped with the dock lines as Tim skillfully eased the vessel away from the pier. One long blast of the ship's whistle signaled his departure, and to Tim's surprise, the captains onshore stood at attention and saluted.

Captain Bill's booming voice echoed over the water: "Live by your ship's name, Captain Tim! Go *Perseverance!*"

Hearing those words, Tim straightened his posture, his heart swelling with purpose. He turned to the bow of the *Perseverance* and steered toward the harbor's mouth, ready to embrace the open sea.

Just as he set his course for the ocean, a smaller boat came into view, slowly making its way across the harbor. Puzzled, Tim watched the vessel inch along behind a channel dredger, which scooped up muck and deposited it into the smaller boat's cargo hold. The sight of the boat tugged at Tim's memory—it looked familiar.

As he crept closer, he spotted the captain lounging on the bridge, feet propped up on the helm, steering the vessel with his feet while chatting on the radio. Tim shook his head, amused, and was about to turn away when the laid-back captain glanced over—and their eyes locked.

Captain Ted

For a moment, Tim didn't recognize the face, but the other captain knew him instantly. Stunned, Captain Ted dropped his radio transmitter, hopped to his feet, and rushed to the starboard bridge wing. His mouth hung open in disbelief as he watched the *Perseverance* glide by.

Tim gave him a slow, deliberate salute, as if to say, *"You made your choice."*

Ted's was the last familiar face Tim saw as he left Hardwork Harbor. A smile crept across his face as he thought about what he'd just witnessed—Ted, Mr. Most Likely to Succeed, now following a dredger, spending his days collecting muck. Tim couldn't help but wonder what excuses Ted offered for how things had turned out.

As the harbor faded behind him, Tim turned his gaze to the horizon, where his bow pointed toward the setting sun and the Big Island of the BYIs. The water stretched wide before him, glimmering with the possibilities of the unknown.

He glanced up at the paddle hanging on the bridge, the same one Captain Peter had given him, a constant reminder of everything it represented. As the wind filled the sails and carried the *Perseverance* forward, Tim heard Captain Peter's voice whisper, clear as day:

"Your course in life is up to you."

HOW TO
GET STARTED

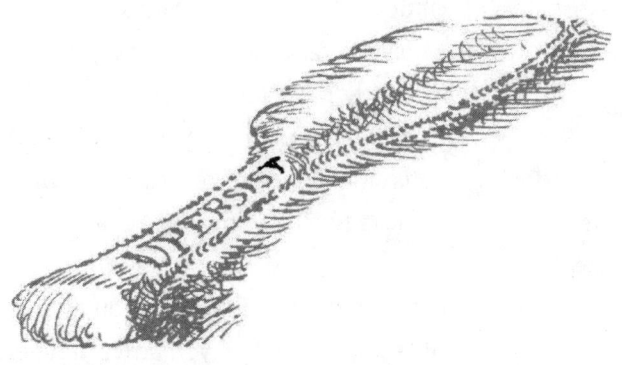

ACTION #8 | TEAM UP!

In the movie *Rambo* Sylvester Stallone plays John Rambo, a soldier who carries out missions alone. However, in SEAL training, instructors constantly remind recruits that SEAL teams are not about lone heroes. They use the phrase "No Rambos" hourly to drive home this point: SEALs never work alone. Each member has a distinct role, and when properly trained and aligned, the team achieves remarkable results. No one is more important than the rest.

Before you can join a SEAL team, you must prove you have the resolve to be there, and one of the ultimate tests for that resolve is Hellweek. For me, it came in the sixth week of my 30-week training. Just hours before Hellweek began, several instructors gave us unforgettable lectures on what it takes to become a SEAL. They shared two powerful metaphors.

The first was from a Vietnam veteran who compared SEAL training to forging a samurai sword: heat the metal, hammer it, cool it in water, and repeat the process 2,000 times. He emphasized that no one could endure such relentless punishment without first knowing why they wanted to be a SEAL. That purpose fuels a trainee's ability to survive the blows.

The second metaphor introduced us to the concept of Rambo: there are no lone wolves in the SEALs. Operating solo isn't just dangerous—it gets people killed. Success comes from unwavering commitment to the team.

From the very first day of training, teamwork is central to everything we do. SEALs train, eat, swim, shoot—even use the bathroom—as a team. The smallest SEAL unit, and the building block for larger teams, is the two-man swim buddy pair. Two swim buddy pairs form a fire team, two fire teams make a squad, and two squads build a platoon. (While today's SEALs use squadrons instead of platoons, the principle remains unchanged: it's all about the team.) Like laying bricks two at a time, SEAL teams are built one swim pair at a time.

Interestingly, your swim buddy doesn't stay with you after graduation. Most graduates join different teams, and when you arrive at a new unit, the process starts over—this time with a new swim buddy who becomes part of a much larger team. Eight pairs come together to form a platoon, which will spend the next two years training for and executing over 150 types of missions. (During my SEAL Team TWO deployment preparation, we trained for 167 different missions.)

Every SEAL team has unique specialties and operates in different environments, but the dynamic remains the same: it all starts with two-man teams, building up to platoons of sixteen men, bonded by purpose, trust, and teamwork.

This same dynamic applies whether you're starting a family or a company—it all begins with finding a "swim buddy." You want someone whose strengths complement your weaknesses. While this sounds simple, the real challenge lies in recognizing and admitting your own weaknesses. It's not easy to acknowledge what you're not good at, but with time, you'll get more comfortable with the idea. It took me a while to accept this myself.

When you're young, you believe you can do it all. But as you encounter excellence in others, you realize you can't excel at everything. For example, I've always been comfortable with public speaking and storytelling, but finance was a different story. I struggled with its language and concepts, even though it's essential for running a successful business. While you should never stop trying to improve in areas that challenge you, it's just as important to acknowledge where you need support. These are the skills to look for in a teammate—someone whose strengths complement your own.

Teammates serve another vital purpose: they can help when you're stuck. A teammate's attitude can mean the difference between success and failure. Not every day on your journey will be easy—some days will be downright tough. There will be times when you question yourself, when nothing seems to go right. On days like these, a great teammate can lift you up.

The challenges that weigh you down might energize your teammate if they align with their natural strengths. Suddenly, an obstacle that had you stumped becomes manageable. And even if neither of you knows the solution, your teammate might know someone who does. Many of my major accomplishments have only been possible because I found great teammates.

First, though, you must find your "why." Great people want to align with a purpose—they need a reason to team up. If you don't have a clear understanding of your why, how can you expect others to see why they should join you? Your why becomes your calling card for attracting the right teammates to help turn your dream into reality. Just like SEAL training demonstrates resolve, understanding your why and showing the progress you've already made proves your commitment. No one wants to join a team destined to fail. People want to be part of a winning effort. When you can clearly articulate your reason for pursuing your dream, you'll inspire others to join you. Finding the perfect teammates starts with a clear understanding of your why.

This is the beauty of the U-PERSIST framework. Once you have a teammate, the actions of U-PERSIST apply all over again. It works just as effectively for teams as it does for individuals, and your teammates will appreciate its structure. Something interesting happens when you build a team: your goals grow. Individual ambitions transform into team goals—and teams tend to dream even bigger. When that happens, you'll need U-PERSIST even more!

No matter your goal, remember that nothing great is ever achieved alone. Period. No one can do it all. Teaming up is essential for accomplishing your dream. It can mean the difference between inaction and incredible success.

It all starts with the first action of U-PERSIST: **Understand your why.** When you know why you're willing to work hard and take risks, you'll inspire others to join your cause. Once you have a teammate, more will follow, and from there, the possibilities are endless.

So, what are you waiting for? Dream as if anything is possible. Dream big—and **GO FOR IT!**

ACKNOWLEDGMENTS

I owe this book to the series of masters and commanders who taught me the Master and Commander Code over the past 45 years. They entered my life at just the right moments to help me with my navigation. They helped me plot a course out of the harbor, rebuild after running aground (sometimes after hitting rocks), and inspired me to modify my ship. They have been there through all the courses I've run in my life, steadfast supporters of my dreams. Without them, the Master and Commander Code wouldn't exist. They represent the best of me. They are:

Jennifer Ryan Mills, wife and teammate. Without her, I would have never left the harbor, got off the rocks, or rebuilt my ship. She's been by my side inspiring me from day one, providing course corrections at just the right moments, battening down the hatches for years on end, and always willing to continue the journey. She and my boys are the best things that have ever happened to me.

Paul and Swan Mills, my parents. They taught me to dream, to believe in myself and use creativity to solve problems. They opened my eyes to art in all its forms, and helped nudge me along the path to appreciate the power of an artistic mindset. Their encouragement, support, and love are what inspired me to choose my own course, to go after my dreams, and to establish my own limits.

Joseph "Pops" Ryan, my father-in-law. He taught me how to make a dream come true. I learned the art of business, the definition of perseverance, and a passion for helping others succeed from him. He continues to teach me the blocking and tackling required to turn a dream into reality, and he and his wife, my mother-in-law, "Mumzie," are the definition of unconditional love and support.

William Hartwell Perry Jr., my crew coach. He was much more than a coach; he was a mentor of boys aspiring to be men. He instilled in me, and hundreds like me, the makings of manhood and how to be a true teammate. He taught me how to pull hard on and off the water, how to win as a team, and no matter what, how to never stop pulling.

My SEAL team, my brotherhood. From my commanding officers to the warrant officers, chiefs, and enlisted men who make everything happen, I learned that limitations are made to be broken, that the power of the team will always prevail over the ego of the individual, and that freedom isn't free. I remain eternally thankful for the men and women who continue the work at the sharpest end of the spear.

Barton O'Brien, entrepreneur. He gave me the inspiration and direction to stay on my course when the winds seemed too strong, the waves too big. He provides radar when I can't see the course in front of me and sonar for those hidden obstacles just below the surface of my courses.

Steve G. Hauser, industrial designer. He taught me much more than form follows function; he showed me how to apply design thinking to more than just products, that the great joys of life come from designing a life worth living, and that even petty officer third class dental techs can achieve greatness!

Michael Cronan, artist. He was much more than a painter, musician, graphic artist, father, and husband. He inspired me to dream bigger while finding purpose within my dreams. He opened my eyes to the poetry of life and the magic of embracing the moment.

Matt Holt, my publisher, Jud "J-Train" Laghi, my agent, and Lydia Choi, my editor, for their consistent encouragement and course corrections. To a crew of remarkable shipmates—Tristram Coburn, Jonathan Eaton, Dan Kirchoff, Brigid Pearson, Barbara Caraballo, Richard Rawson, and John Ross Bush—who were the experts and captains I needed to make this dream come true. Thank you, Tris, Jon, Dan, Brigid, Barbara, Richard, and John—I'd go to sea with you again any day!

And finally, and most profoundly, my boys—Henry, Charlie, John, and William. I wrote this book over ten years of late nights and long flights. I used the code to accomplish this Milestone Goal. My "why" was clear: it was for you. I know of no greater "why" than the purpose of helping the next generation stand on our shoulders to make future generations better. Mom and I don't expect you to follow our course; we want you to follow your own courses. Your courses, your dreams, are entirely Up To You. You decide your journeys and your destinations. Just know we'll be there every step of the way, cheering you to Go For It! Dream big, work hard, have fun, and Never, Ever Give Up on your dreams. We love you.

ABOUT THE AUTHOR

Photo by Kathleen Harrison

Alden M. Mills has set a course to help 100 million people achieve their own milestone goals. He believes if he can help others do more than they originally thought possible that their confidence will exponentially inspire millions more to do the same. He developed his strategy for success while becoming a rowing champion, a Navy SEAL platoon commander, and the creator and co-founder of Perfect Fitness, producer of the Perfect Pushup and other fitness products and Inc. 500's fastest-growing consumer-product company in 2009. His company earned over 40 patents worldwide and has sold more than 20 million units from his ideas. He is the author of two other bestselling books: *Unstoppable Teams* and *Unstoppable Mindset*. His appearances include the *Today* show, the *Donny Deutsch Show*, and the *CBS Mornings* show, and Perfect Pushups have been featured on *The Biggest Loser*, *Conan*, *The Tonight Show with Jay Leno*, *The Big Idea*, and *Late Night with Jimmy Fallon*, and have been endorsed by Simon Cowell, Brian Urlacher, Jamie Foxx, Dwayne Howard, and many others. When he is not traveling the world working with organizations to help them be unstoppable, he spends every waking moment with his friends and family on or by the water. Alden lives in Marin County with his wife, four sons, and two Labradors.